The

# Physician's Covenant

# The
# Physician's Covenant

## Images of the Healer
## in Medical Ethics

*second edition*

WILLIAM F. MAY

Westminster John Knox Press
Louisville, Kentucky

Book design by Sharon Adams
Cover design by Night & Day Design

Second edition
Published by Westminster John Knox Press
Louisville, Kentucky

This book is printed on acid-free paper that meets the American National Standards Institute Z39.48 standard. ∞

PRINTED IN THE UNITED STATES OF AMERICA

00 01 02 03 04 05 06 07 08 09 — 10 9 8 7 6 5 4 3 2 1

**Library of Congress Cataloging-in-Publication Data**
May, William F.
    The physician's covenant: images of the healer in medical
ethics
        p. cm.
    Includes bibliographic references and index.
    ISBN 0-664-22274-9 (alk. paper)
        1. Medical ethics. 2. Medical personnel and patient.
    3. Healing—Moral and ethical aspects. I. Title.

R725.5 .M38 2000
174'.2—dc21                                        00-040855

*In memory of*

Harry Stuart May
1903–1969

*and*

Leontine May
1902–1996

# Contents

# Preface to the Second Edition

The several images of the healer explored in the first edition of *The Physician's Covenant* continue to shape medical practice, but this second edition adds new material on several issues. The Introduction now responds to the resurgent interest in religion and health and explores the controversy surrounding the current efforts to link piety with good health and longevity. The chapter on the physician as fighter notes the developments in genetic screening and counseling, genome mapping, and genetic engineering (somatic and germ line) that promise eventually to expand the medical fight against disease and death. However, the chapter also examines at greater length the movements for assisted suicide and euthanasia, which have power-fully opposed the effort to define medicine exclusively by a resistance to death. The chapter on the physician as covenant-partner with the patient expands further the differences between the covenantal image and the current tendency, in both fee-for-service medicine and managed care, to see the doctor-patient exchange sim-ply as a commercial contract. I have also added a final, new chapter on the health care system; this chapter grows out of my work in spring 1993 in Washington, D.C., on the ethical foundations for health care reform.

A society needs not only covenanted practitioners— physicians and nurses—and covenanted institutions— hospitals and clinics—but also a health care system that supports and sustains faithful medical practice and that offers universal access and a comprehensive range of services at a level the nation can afford to sustain.

In part, these newer materials draw on lectures I gave at the Institute of Religion at the Texas Medical Center, at the invitation of its former director, Dr. Allen D. Verhey, and are published here with the permission of Jon Pott, Vice President and Editor-in-Chief of Wm. B. Eerdmans Publishing Company, who printed those lectures under the title *Testing the Medical Covenant* (1996).

This second edition of *The Physician's Covenant* issues with my thanks to G. Nick Street of Westminster John Knox Press, who has encouraged it, and to Oleg Makariev, my administrative assistant, whose research help and critical judgment on this and other of my projects have allowed me to respond to the invitation from the Press. I am also grateful to Cary M. Maguire, who generously established the chair I have held at Southern Methodist University since 1985.

The first edition of this book carried a dedication to my parents now deceased. That dedication still stands. But, as my parents would recognize, Beverly May has sustained me in all that I have been able to undertake.

William F. May

Cary M. Maguire Professor of Ethics
Southern Methodist University

# Acknowledgments

Any illusions an author may harbor about his independence fade on the day he sits down to tote up his debts and write his acknowledgments. My list of benefactors is long; the gifts received are substantial.

An Open Faculty Fellowship from the Lilly Endowment, Inc., 1976–77, allowed me to spend a year as an observer at the New York Hospital. A longtime friend and colleague, Dr. Eric J. Cassell of the Cornell Medical College, served as my host there. "Pete" MacDonald of the National Endowment for the Humanities invited me to teach month-long seminars for five summers to health care practitioners. These seminars gave me extended contact with a sensitive group of physicians, surgeons, nurses, social workers, physical therapists, and other professionals in the field. Some of them, including Dr. Dan English and Dr. Gary Burke, have read portions of this work. Long ago, Vincent F. Torczynski, M.D., gave me some sense of exemplary practice.

Dr. Daniel Callahan, Executive Director of the Hastings Center, and Professor William Lee Miller, then Director of the Poynter Center, Indiana University, encouraged my writing and research during the many years that I carried administrative responsibilities at Indiana University. I am also grateful to the University for the deferred maintenance it bestowed on this former administrator under a generous leave program, 1976–77 and 1978–79.

From 1980 to 1985, I served as Senior Research Scholar at the Kennedy Institute of Ethics, Georgetown University. I enjoyed favorable conditions there among excellent colleagues—in a chair endowed by the Kennedy Foundation and named for the head of a distinguished American family, Joseph P. Kennedy Sr. The position also afforded me contact with Eunice Kennedy Shriver and Sargent Shriver, whose keen interest in ethics has inspirited the work of many.

Colleagues who have not read this work but to whom I am deeply indebted include the late Paul Ramsey, whose early course work in Christian ethics at Princeton University led to my vocational choice; and my long-standing and valued colleague at Indiana University, Professor David H. Smith, now chair of the Department of Religious Studies there.

Most writers keep in mind a short list of professionals whose cold eyes they would like to please and whose blue pencils they respect. Two friends, the aforementioned William Lee Miller and, in this instance especially, Adolf L. Soens, Associate Professor of English at the University of Notre Dame, have favored me with their stern judgments. Professor Soens closely scanned the penultimate draft, thereby helping me make the book better than it was while letting it be what it is.

The manuscript has emerged through several drafts, with earlier and shorter versions of Chapters 2 and 4 appearing respectively under the titles "The Right to Die and the Obligation to Care," in *Death and Decision*, American Association for the Advancement of Science Selected Symposium 18, ed. by Ernan McMullen (Westview Press, 1978), and "Code, Covenant, Contract, or Philanthropy," *Hastings Center Report* 5 (December 1975). I am also thankful to James Heaney, Ph.D., editor at The Westminster Press, for nudging me to write this book and for bold editorial judgment.

In the workshop itself, I am indebted to Emilie Dolge, who has given thorough and highly intelligent care to the preparation of the manuscript through its several drafts; to Mimi Herrmann, who has proofread some of the drafts; and to Rev. Abigail Rian Evans, a Ph.D. student in Bioethics who serves as my research associate. In addition to her research assistance on this volume, Mrs. Evans has supported my work across a two-year period, in countless ways and beyond my deserving, and also secured further support from an anonymous donor. To these two women, named and unnamed, I owe much.

Personally, I acknowledge with pride and gratitude Catherine May, M.D., who may recognize some of her comments now and then in the text, and Beverly May, New York actress, who has served as the fixed star in my life across thirty-two years—in the midst of all the craziness and improvisation of a commuting marriage.

# Introduction

The task of ethics in the professional setting might be called, at least in part, corrective vision. The metaphor of vision links ethics with some form of knowledge, as does the etymological link between sight and insight. The philosophical and religious traditions of the West have long connected seeing and knowing. Plato relied on the metaphor of vision, when, in the myth of the cave, he likened the movement from ignorance to knowledge to the painful ascent from the darkness of a cave into the blinding glare of the sun, the idea of the Good. The classical theological tradition similarly linked ethics and religion with insight when it defined as the chief end of humankind seeing God in the beatific vision. Although the Protestant Reformers emphasized the political metaphor of establishing the kingdom of God more than the noetic metaphor of seeing God, Calvin held strongly to the cognitive element in faith and obedience. The metaphor of vision has carried forward into the modern university setting whenever the university reaffirms that ethics in the classroom should not seek to bend the will or manipulate feelings, but to illuminate the understanding.

The vision, however, that concerns the ethicist differs from the vision available to the senses or through the instruments of science. Ethics supplies a type of *corrective* lens. Ethics relies heavily on the distinction between what is and what ought to be. Such corrective vision, however, challenges not so much the world the descriptive sciences see as the world distorted through the bias of institutional structures or through the prism of human imperfection and vice.

To identify corrective vision as the goal of ethics hardly flatters the faculty of reason. On the contrary, it freely acknowledges the possibility of reason's distortion, of which professional myopia exemplifies but one of the milder forms. Professional preoccupation produces merely a kind of heedlessness about goals. More seriously, vision distorts as people begin to offer a warped view of the world in order to justify their behavior. Immoral behavior seduces by presenting itself as plausible. It usually presents itself as world-compliant rather than world-defiant. Theologians call this deformed but appealing vision temptation; lay people call it rationalization. No one is so much the scoundrel as not to think of his or her behavior as justified. Malicious persons hate because they believe that enemies out there justify that hatred. Avaricious persons assume that they must deal ruthlessly with their competitors, because a dog-eat-dog world demands it; otherwise, they won't be able to educate their children. The Nixon people sought to invoke that plausibility with the phrases "at that point in time" or "in that time frame." They explained their behavior as corresponding to the pressures and imperatives of the world as it is rather than as defying it.

Even more disconcerting, a warped vision of the world and our duties within it not only justifies aberrant behavior but also helps alter the world to conform to the warp. People who hate because they believe that they have enemies out there whom they must hate provoke, in due course, such enemies even if they were not there in the first place. A self-deceiving vision of the world is demiurgic. It helps manufacture a world that conforms to the unlovely picture it paints. Physicians who practice defensive medicine, ordering massive tests for little more reason than to protect their own hides, make no small contribution to the rapid rise in the costs of health care, which in turn engenders the resentful willingness of patients to bring malpractice suits, against which the physicians sought to protect themselves in the first place.

Moral reflection attempts, at its best, a knowledgeable revisioning of the world that human practice presents. Corrective vision of this sort offers an immensely practical freedom. We cannot change our behavior unless, in some respects, our perception of the world also changes. In this task, the ethicist theorizes—literally—and thus helps liberate. Unfortunately, theorizing suggests to the practical person a remote and abstract enterprise, lacking in relevance and payoff, blindly distant from the world of practice. But classically understood, the theorist provides a fresh and liberating vision of the world. So Plato understood it when he cast the *polis* that he knew in the light of the ideal state. So Machiavelli implied when, in the dedication to *The Prince*, he compared the political theorist to the landscape painter who views the world from the distance of insight and perspective. And so Calvin understood theological ethics when he once called the Holy Spirit the "spectacles of faith." The word "theory" in its Greek root refers to vision. Appropriately, the word "theater" is also related to *theōria*, because theater, like good theory, presents us with a world to see and frees us from the local and given. Thus, applied ethics has a theoretical component related to liberating insight and vision.

So conceived, moral reflection does not merely scan the world as it is or prepare leaders for the professions as they are. Rather, it entails a knowledgeable re-visioning of foundations and ends. Through this cognitive illumination, it serves, in some limited way, the human capacity for resolution and decision. Ethical theory may not always eliminate moral quandaries, but it opens up a wider horizon in which they may be seen for what they are and thus become other than they were. It helps correct our perceptions of the world as it appears to the myopia of timidity and the astigmatism of vice. To this degree, it helps us serve the worlds in which we work, not perfectly but well.

## The Role of Images in Corrective Vision

Most modern theorizing about the moral life seems extraordinarily abstract. It seeks to interpret particular problems and cases by appeal to general moral principles that provide solutions to quandaries. This book takes a different tack. It explores the pervasive role of images, particularly of metaphors, in understanding the healer's role and defining his or her tasks.

The word "image," of course, conveys a variety of social meanings. It can mean a role expectation or a socially enforced model (the image of the sovereign in Victorian England). It can refer to a powerfully internalized self-perception, the way one sees oneself when one looks deeply in the mirror. In the world of Madison Avenue, "image" separates from substance; it becomes one of the many possible public projections behind which politicians, companies, and movie stars can conveniently operate. Images sometimes point to the similarities between an original and its reflection (she's the image of her mother) or spring from the juxtaposed dissimilarities of a metaphor (the idea dawned on me). In the latter senses, images help us to perceive and express what we perceive. Images give continuity to time by helping us to retrieve the past and chart the future. Without the help of images, we could not "make present" in the now, what is no longer and what is not yet. Without the service of images, we would be condemned to the instant. Overriding images shape and order our experience and present us with the imperatives by which we live.

This book does not escape the variety of these overlapping meanings, although it deals chiefly with metaphors (such as parent and technician) which shape the healer's sense of the world in which he or she must function and define the corresponding professional role. Such metaphors, of course, might conceivably come from two sources, one of them literary. We celebrate the talent of the poet or novelist who strikes off a phrase that juxtaposes two entities so as to give us a fresh understanding of both. Such literary metaphors do not merely ornament. They develop a cognitive significance, a potential for corrective vision. For example, the novelist Nelson Algren in the simile "Chicago is like an old girl friend with a broken nose" juxtaposes two dissimilars and yet says something about affectionate, bruising, guilt-ridden relationships to a city and to a woman that he could not express apart from the juxtaposition.

The images and metaphors that chiefly occupy us pervade ordinary behavior and speech. The physician's freedom with first names and body contact signals a parental understanding of the healer's role. The white lab coat points to the scientific origin of medical authority and hints at the technician, the body mechanic, at work. The title "doctor," from its root, implies teaching, whereas the term "professional," in root, suggests the notion of a covenant, a declaration or vow to be faithful for something to someone. Finally, the language of war dominates the modern understanding of disease and shapes the professional's response. The heart suffers an attack; cancers invade and spread like a conquering army; researchers look for a magic bullet. The military metaphor lurks within even the relatively pallid "immunize," which, etymologically, means to render neutral a belligerent.

An image tells a compressed story, not a particular story about an identifiable person or an exemplary tale designed to inspire, but a prototypical story to which all specific narratives bear a family resemblance. The prototypical image of the physician as parent or fighter functions in a fashion roughly comparable to what producers in the media call a "bible" for a television show. The "bible" provides a basic framework for every show, a general conception of character and a sketch of structural relations to other characters and circumstances that allow a writer to map out what fits with that character and what jars. For example, physicians who perceive their profession as defined by a fight against death would be unlikely to "pull the plug." Physicians with a parental understanding of their role would likely take great care in how they tell the truth to a patient. Basic images or metaphors supply compressed but powerful stories, prototypical for the stories that practitioners themselves write as they fashion their own deeds, works, careers, and justifications.

In its cognitive aspect, an image for the healer provides, first, a definition of social role, a specification of the office, as it were, of the healer. The images to be covered in this book derive partly from the healing activity itself. They also derive partly from other human activities—parenting, fighting, covenanting, and teaching. In this case, the image is largely metaphorical. It juxtaposes two different activities and interprets one through the other.[1] The metaphor, in this event, works heuristically in both directions. To insist that the healer must teach says something not only about healing but also about the sometimes-therapeutic impact of teaching. Finally, images for the healer derive partly from notions of godly action. In the background of the Greek concept of the work of the healer loom the goddess Hygeia and the god Asclepius, who authorize, respectively, the preventive and curative aspects of medicine. Behind the other human images of the parent, fighter, covenanter, and teacher loom, respectively, notions of God as Father (less often in the West as Mother), King, Partner, and Prophet.

When these religious aspects of the image come to the fore, one begins to explore not only metaphorical but also analogical ranges of meaning. In these instances, one interprets the specific activity of healing not only through other human activities but also against the background of a divine activity. This divine activity develops a complicated analogical relation to its human counterpart. God's "parenting" both authorizes and provides warrant for human parenting, but it also provides a model for criticism of human parenting. To call God King authorizes human governing but also provides a severe standard by which to measure the human exercise of governing. The divine activity justifies, teaches, and encourages imitation, but it also judges, chastens, and disciplines all human discharge of the role (a fact that both conservatives and radicals have failed to notice). We do not always find ourselves, in our moral criticism of an image (such as parenting), seeking for a standpoint outside the image, but engage in some analogical leaps within the image itself.

An image provides more than a definition of social role; it also lays bare a metaphysical setting in which people act out the "bible" of their lives, their basic script. The picture of the physician as parent or fighter presupposes a sense of the human condition, the goods that favor and the evils that threaten men and women, the powers that hover at the foot of the sickbed. Images touch on the metaphysical; they condense the ultimate; they lay bare the human plight and prospect.

This metaphysical horizon also provides a limiting silhouette for one's understanding of the moral agent. It shapes responses that befit the professional who must choose whether to succor as a parent; to fight like a mercenary; to find refuge in technical competence; to covenant with the stranger; or also to teach patients whom pain disorients and uncertainty baffles.

Patients, of course, also figure differently in these images. The prototypical story describes the basic character not only of the hero but also of those with whom he or she deals and the social setting in which the story plays itself out. The parental physician perceives the patient as a child; the fighter, an embattled city; the technician, a body convertible into charts and lab values; the covenanter, a bonded partner in the pursuit of health; the teacher, a student distracted by pain and uncertainty. Further, an institution that perceives itself as a fighter against death tends to imitate the military camp; it also relies heavily on the rhetoric of war to secure a growing share of the GNP.

As a guide to practice, images function differently from moral principles, and they imply somewhat different views of the moral agent. Philosophical ethics, as usually taught, orients less to image than to principles; it presupposes not the ordinary volume of work with which the practitioner must cope but the exceptional case. It assumes that the practitioner is riddled with uncertainty in facing a particular decision and seeks help from the ethicist in identifying the right set of principles to resolve the quandary.[2] (Some ethicists and clinicians have so honored this view of medical ethics that they considered publishing a book on the subject that would fit into the physician's hip pocket for the handy resolution of quandaries.) Images do not function quite so successfully in those situations that the moralists call hard cases. They do not operate as a manual for getting the decision maker out of an exceptional moral bind in which he or she does not know what to do. Rather, they provide a comprehensive ordering of life—an interpretation of role, metaphysical setting, and institutional context—that makes moral behavior seem more like a rite repeated than a puzzle solved. An image provides a compelling picture of the world and one's role in it. What one does appears to be what the world compels. The image renders another kind of behavior unthinkable.

This sense of the moral life sets a few traps. Merely living by metaphors tends to exclude moral criticism rather than to invite it. An image often rationalizes a given pattern of activity rather than subjecting it to rational criticism. Metaphors can deceive: The physician can win only a few firefights in the battle against death, but the full-dress military metaphor holds out the prospect of winning the war. Images, moreover, carry a demiurgic power that compounds the difficulty.

Metaphors are demiurgic in the sense that they do not simply describe the world; they partly create and re-create the world to conform to an image. When we perform a role in a specific way, we cue others about the way we expect them to play, and when they so behave, we find confirmation of our original perform-ance. The parental physician encourages dependence in patients, which in turn justifies his or her behaving paternalistically. This demiurgic power of an image extends beyond the social level. Uncannily, the all-out military counterattack with antibiotics against invasive bacteria has tended to generate new bacteria immune to the weapons of attack. These bacteria seem to behave like an enemy that adapts to the tactics of coun-terattack. This development in turn encourages the society to entrench itself even further in treating health as a military objective. What, then, generates moral criticism of images?

First, the image itself. The image establishes a stan-dard that judges both defective and corrupt versions of performance. Parenting, for example, demands a readiness to expend oneself for one's children. Self-expenditure should characterize the physician who interprets the task of healing parentally. This standard of self-expending care criticizes the performance of abusive physicians who exercise authority over their patients, but for their own sake, not for the good of their charges. Again, the military image highlights tactical cunning as an important and legitimate fea-ture of the healer's task. But the military image pres-ents a number of alternative forms of the heroic life. World War II, for example, offered figures as differ-ent as Generals Bradley, MacArthur, Montgomery, and Patton. Bradley came to symbolize a commitment to technical excellence and teamwork and a respect for civilian control. MacArthur displayed technical virtuosity but also bridled under civilian authority. Montgomery acquired a reputation for tactical brilliance but had a vanity that clouded his judgment in collaborative enterprises. Patton exhibited a legendary daring and energy that led to incomparable boldness on the field but also to a troubling mysticism about war and a Caesarian view of military command. All of these possibilities in the basic image of the military surface as well in medical practice. The Pattons and the MacArthurs among M.D.s insist on a comprehensive and terminal authority and tend not to see the modest tactical limits of the struggle. The Montgomerys of the hospital floor serve vanity and image somewhat more than cause. And the Bradleys seem a somewhat more attractive alternative, mixing competence and teamwork and a sense for the limits of authority.

Moral reflection requires, additionally, criticism of the image itself. What features of healing does a particular image emphasize? What other features does it obscure? Whenever one interprets one activity through the medium of another, the second both highlights and hides the first.[3] Some features of healing stand out more vividly as refracted through a particular image; others recede into the background and become neglected. The military image highlights the curative aspects of medicine, but it woefully neglects the tasks of preventive, rehabilitative, and chronic care. The parental image highlights the profound responsibilities that the patient's neediness, misery, and dependence generate, but it tends to obscure the adult patient who hides in the patient-as-child and who finally demands respect. Thus criticism of the image itself must take place.

But criticism of the image is not itself image free. The agenda of this book is not the destruction of images. The iconoclast cannot wholly escape them. Philosophical criticism of the parental image, for example, largely emerges in the name of the patient's autonomy. But the word "autonomy" itself originated in a political metaphor. The Greek terms *auto* (self) and *nomos* (law or norms) refer to governance according to the self's own laws or norms—an ideal prized by the Greek city-states in their effort to be self-governing communities. This political metaphor later shifted in meaning with the rise of classical liberal politics in the nineteenth century, which associated the self with an expansive and indeterminate liberty free of any and all constraints, external and internal. Moral argument almost never goes on at a level utterly free of image and metaphor. As Lakoff and Johnson have pointed out, the interpretation of reasoning itself is rife with metaphor—as in winning an argument (the metaphor of fighting) and constructing a case (the metaphor of building).[4]

This book therefore does not march through a half-dozen metaphors only to criticize them all from a moral point of view beyond all images. Its center of gravity rests in the image of the healer as covenanter, the central inclusive image for the whole. That image appears early in the Western theological tradition. It centers in the covenants between God and humankind, which the Scriptures gather up into a canon, and which are designated the Old and New Covenants. But the image itself also springs from ancient political precedent in the treaties between political powers and in the vows of marriage, friendship, and professional relationships. The Hippocratic Oath, according to modern scholarship, also defines covenantally the obligations of a young physician to his teacher and his teacher's family. In Puritan society, the term "covenant" dominated the understanding of community both ecclesiastically and politically; and William Faulkner, the novelist, presented a fictional world in which the same, essentially biblical, covenant between men and women with one another and with the land shapes human life. The image of the covenanter also informs this work.

But the existence of a central image for this book does not altogether dismiss the other images. They have a place and function within the whole not unlike the continuing role of lesser symbols in Paul Ricoeur's *The Symbolism of Evil.*[5] In that work, the philosopher explored four competing symbols for the interpretation of evil—tragic, Gnostic, dualistic, and biblical. Ricoeur concluded that the biblical symbol best accounted for evil. But after reaching that conclusion, he raised the important question of whether this judgment deprived the other symbols of all value. He concluded, finally, that it did not. The other three symbols helpfully pointed to aspects of evil, which, though acknowledged by the superior symbol, would likely slip into obscurity apart from the highlighting that the other three symbols offered. Correspondingly, the covenantal image accommodates in principle the healer's activities; it warrants them all. But alone the image does not throw important features of the healer's task into sufficient relief. The images of parent, fighter, technician, and teacher still clarify.

We should not expect, finally, a perfect harmonization of the images at all levels of inference. Comparing Chicago to an old girlfriend with a broken nose does not square in every detail with Carl Sandburg's description of Chicago as the "city of the big shoulders." Yet both metaphors say something important about that city. Lakoff and Johnson have observed that metaphors should not scrupulously correspond in all details.[6] The images of fighter and teacher sometimes contradict each other. But these images can also supplement each other and find their harmonizing context in still a third. Metaphors do support one another in coherent patterns upon which vision and behavior depend. They can thus serve to correct our vision.

A somewhat condescending attitude toward images, metaphors, and stories shows up in the philosophical tradition as it attempts (at its most sympathetic) to assess the place of religion in the moral life. Religion generally, and the Western religious tradition in particular, places a heavy emphasis on narrative events (Exodus-Mt. Sinai, death-resurrection, the flight to Mecca) and all their attendant images (king, parent, shepherd, liberator, and the like) used to define both God's action and fitting human response to that action. Philosophers at best tend to reduce religious narratives to rhetorical illustrations of those principles to which reason already holds. They cannot imagine particular sacred narratives as opening up a horizon against which the believer can see silhouetted the commands, rules, virtues, and principles (and sometimes even the relative weight of those principles) that govern his or her life. Immanuel Kant, for example, prized Jesus' sacrificial life simply as an illustration of moral principles otherwise known. Jesus' life inspired and instructed, but presumably one can directly grasp the principle independent of the story. Thus religion, at the most and at its best, embodies morality for people who do not have a direct, philosophical grasp of principles; it offers principles heightened and warmed up by inspiring example. It does not imagine the power of sacred story itself to ground the principle and perhaps also to expose its limits.

This book, then, differs from conventional work in medical ethics. Most philosophers and theologians writing about medical ethics work either as secular moralists, or, at most, as closet Christians and Jews. If they have religious convictions (or expertise), they systematically suppress these resources when they write on the subject—and for culturally understand-able reasons. They perceive that the society at large and the professions in particular are confessionally indeterminate. Professionals also offer their services to religiously varied populations of strangers. With few exceptions, we do not expect or want to see a Reform Jewish, a Presbyterian, or an Eastern Ortho-dox version of medical practice. Hence moralists are also reluctant to write as Christians and Jews.

While culturally understandable, this response, in my judgment, mistakenly diagnoses our times. For bet-ter or worse, the modern world reeks of religion. These religious forces do not always, or even for the most part, conform to official Judaism and Christianity, but they pervade our times and, not least, those fateful events that attend sickness, suffering, and death. These events shatter or suspend the ordinary resources that people trust for managing their lives and send them to the doctor in hope of rescue. They clothe the doctor accordingly in the images of shelter and rescue—the parent, the fighter, and others. The full power of these images, and their hold over the layperson and therefore the professional, does not become fully clear unless we recognize the deep religious apprehensions that give rise to these images. We must see them, at least in part, in their religious setting.

## The Shaman: Forerunner to the Images

Medicine men and women or shamans in traditional societies foreshadow several of the images that shape medical practice to this day. As shamans engage in healing, they do so in the setting of a religious narrative. Strange myths accompanied their manipulations and account both for illness and the effectiveness of their power. At first glance, modern medicine seems far removed from this world of religious myth. We think of ourselves as the children of a secular, scientific age. But looking at the shaman's work in its religious reverberations suggests that latent religious forces are still at work in contemporary medicine, religious forces that shape the perceptions and responses that men and women oppose to the crushing power of disease, suffering, and death.

In traditional societies (both ancient and those still surviving), sacred power communicates itself to the members of society through those who bear its marks: priests, prophets, shamans, and kings foremost among them. They represent power that possesses them as instruments through which it imparts itself to the community. This power fills the priest and drives him to lead the community in its worship; it fills the king and drives him to govern; it possesses the prophet and drives him to foretell the future, advise, and forewarn; and it drives shamans to teach, guide, harmonize, and heal. These analytically distinct offices often combine in a given traditional society. Kings and priests exercise power regularly and relatively permanently, but prophets and shamans depend on a more episodic bestowal of power, which they receive during a special state of ecstasy.[7]

Shamans (like their descendants in still-surviving traditional societies) often combined three functions:

curing the sick, directing communal sacrifice, and escorting the dead to the other world. They combined, in effect, three offices that have been separated in modern times: physician, priest, and undertaker. As priest, they helped to harmonize the community with the powers that be. A special talent for ecstasy linked their further two roles as healer and undertaker. "Ecstasy" means standing outside oneself. Correspondingly, shamans-to-be underwent an initiation rite in which they subjected themselves to a period of wandering, dreaming, madness, or sickness—all ecstatic states.[8] Clearly, the wanderer, the dreamer, and the madman stand "beside themselves," but so also does the sick person, and not simply for the physiological reason that a person in the throes of a high fever gives the impression of being out of his or her head.

The shamanic myth in its dominant form explains sickness as a state in which the soul of the sick person has departed from the body. Either the soul has strayed from the village or lost its natural harmony with the world and the gods, or demons have stolen it and imprisoned it in another world. All illness, in effect, springs from a loss of soul, a withdrawal of the *animus,* that is, of the animating power or vitalizing principle apart from which the dispirited body withers and decays. Given this understanding of illness, shamans as healers must, perforce, work through ecstasy. They must have the special knack of going beyond themselves, tracking after a departed soul, and retrieving it; thereby, they restore sick persons to health.

This special ecstatic power also enables shamans to function as undertakers. When death occurs, shamans must again go beyond themselves from the land of the living, but, this time, to escort a departed soul to its final lodging place among the dead. Thus a talent for ecstasy enables both the healer's work of retrieval and the undertaker's work of disposal. Our culture, of course, has separated the two offices. The doctor and the undertaker stand distinct in our specialized culture, partly for pragmatic reasons, but also for important symbolic reasons. We would feel somewhat distraught if we discovered that the physician whom we expected to duel with disease and death ran the funeral parlor next door.

The shamanic myth, in the main, interprets disease and healing through the metaphor of the loss and recovery of positive power. However, a minor motif in the myth suggests a second, more negative, interpretation of disease. In some versions of the myth, the soul, in the course of its wandering, falls into the grasp of demonic power. Emphasis on this detail of the story suggests that disease results not so much from the loss of a positive, but from the assault of a negative, power. Correspondingly, the therapist must do battle with those negative and destructive forces that hold the sick person in their grip. The therapist is fighter more than retriever and caretaker. In this second narrative, then, one must reckon with two dimensions of sacred power: first, the demonic destructive power against which the shaman struggles, and, second, whatever power of healing he brings to bear in that struggle.

## The Myth Still Lives

These opposing views of the healer persist to this day. One tradition views disease primarily as the *absence* of health or of those positive powers that provide health—food, sun, rest, exercise, and the balanced energies of the psyche. Correspondingly, the therapist must put the patient in contact once again with those life-giving and health-giving powers. This positive definition of the healing task characterizes such divergent therapists as the ancient shaman, who "retrieves" the wandering soul of the sick person; the physician caretaker, who prescribes for his or her patients a regimen that affords them a balanced life and diet; the social reformer of the nineteenth century, who sought to put city people in touch with the life-giving properties of food, sun, and clean water; and the modern apologist who, like Leon Kass, argues that medicine should aim, not chiefly at preventing suffering and death, but at sustaining health.[9]

Alternatively interpreted, disease springs, not from the absence of positive powers and order, but from the incursion of negative, invasive, and destructive forces. This negative theory of disease operates in the demonism of the ancient world and reappears in modern medicine with the identification of bacteria and viruses that wreak havoc in the body. Today, the interpretation of disease as invasive power dominates and defines the physician's role as fighter and confers on physicians quasi-military authority over all other health care practitioners; and it authorizes budgetary support for the armamentarium of drugs and procedures with which physicians fight against disease and death, with the hospital as their chosen battlefield.

Today, of course, we find ourselves in a somewhat disconcerting end stage for both kinds of medical practice. Pessimism prevails. The first type of medicine enjoins us to use natural powers and to recover health through an abundance of food, sun, water, and air. But today, suspicion vitiates these traditional sources of strength. The water of New Orleans clogs the arteries; the sun gives us a precancerous glow; and

food—at least the all-American breakfast, some say—
is chock full of poison.

The second, more aggressive type of medicine
shows a destructive underside, the fashionable term
for which is iatrogenic illness. The magic bullet no
longer charms; it has its dangerous side effects. It
strikes not only the disease but its host. We fight
destructive powers by mobilizing forces that are
themselves dangerous and destructive. Consequently,
we react either by rejecting the medical establishment
in favor of lay medicine in a somewhat anxious, narcissistic, and hypochondriacal milieu, or by surren-
dering ourselves even further to the hands of the
expert, on the grounds that battles against transcen-
dental evil require green berets.

## Contemporary Religion and the Myth of Restoration

Toward the end of the twentieth century, a large
body of literature surfaced on the subject of religion
and healing; this literature hearkens back to the first
of the two ancient forms of the shamanic myth. It
thrives on images of healing as restoration to positive
power and the beneficial role of religion in securing
that restoration. Dr. Herbert Benson, author of the
widely read *Relaxation Response*,[10] implicitly relies on
the ancient story line with the phrase "remembered
wellness." He urges on his readers a variety of religious and quasi-religious practices and beliefs—the
relaxation response, remembered wellness, spirituality, biofeedback, church attendance, healing services,
twelve steps, intercessory prayer, power and biology
of belief, focus words, wired for God, and faith factor.[11] Although these beliefs and practices should not

replace the medical treatment of disease, they provide a major resource, Benson argues, in the larger agenda of healing.[12]

In a comprehensive review of the literature on "the faith factor," Matthews, Larson, and Barry similarly claim that religion produces positive health benefits in reducing nicotine and drug use, reducing depression and blood pressure, improving the quality of life in cancer and heart patients, and increasing survival rates.[13] Such religious practice and belief do not constitute an alternative to medicine; they do not eliminate the need for medications, surgery, and other procedures; however, they offer a major strategy in preventative, rehabilitative, and long-term care. Consequently, clinicians should recognize spirituality as an "important medical tool" in developing therapeutic regimens for patients.[14]

A counterattack, on both empirical and moral grounds, against those who advocate the use of spirituality as a medical tool appeared in the influential medical journal *The Lancet* in 1999. Empirically, R. P. Sloan and colleagues argue, the studies that report a causal link between religion and health are faulty. They fail to control for confounding factors, "such as behavioral and genetic differences and for stratification variables, such as age, sex, education, ethnicity, socio-economic status, and health status."[15] Thus these studies give a misleading impression of the causal association of religion with health. Religion may lead some people to healthful behaviors and habits—eating, drinking, and sexual—but not invariably. Moreover, such habits may be acquired in other ways. Morally, *The Lancet* authors complain, the recommendation (by Matthews and colleagues) that physicians ask patients what they can do as their doctors "to support their faith or religious commitment" departs from established medical expertise and therefore abuses professional status. Furthermore, such overtures may actually harm patients by implying that their illness results from their moral failure.

I can only partly agree with these critics of the role of religion. They have appropriately drawn attention to the empirical inadequacies of many studies linking patient health with religious beliefs and practices. However, from John Wesley forward, scholars in the West have noted a link between religiously inspired discipline and good health habits.[16] To correlate with health, religion need not be the sole, inevitable, or sufficient cause of good habits. *The Lancet* authors have also justifiably raised questions about clinicians who might arouse in patients a sense of moral failure. Tactlessness in the sick room is always out of place and often cruel. However, spiritual resources can help patients rise to their responsibilities for self-care; and self-care can be an important ingredient in preventative, rehabilitative, long-term, and even terminal care. *The Lancet* criticism calls for professional discretion and tact rather than avoidance. Clinicians may tactfully help patients husband their full range of resources in maintaining their health or refer them to other professionals or laypeople competent to offer such help.

My chief objection to the current literature on religion and health is religious rather than empirical or moral. The literature sometimes caters to a narcissism in the believer and thus runs the risk of instrumentalizing and therefore trivializing God. First, too much of the literature on the role of religion in healing focuses too narrowly on the afflicted believer and his or her immediate circle of family and friends. In medical crisis, Scripture certainly authorizes believers to pray and to intercede for help: "Father, let this cup pass from me . . ." But the afflicted and their company of relatives and friends should also pray within a discipline that pares away all narcissism—". . . nevertheless, not my will but thine be done." A narrow focus on one's own plight can overlook the broader reach of intercessory prayer as it extends beyond one's circle of intimates toward the stranger and the forlorn. Such prayer implies a wider religious responsibility for health care. The church spaciously acts on the full scope of intercessory prayer when, in addition to specific prayers for healing, it also founds and supports hospitals; inspires doctors, nurses, social workers, and chaplains vocationally; develops institutions such as hospices, drug addiction programs, and medical self-help organizations; and tackles social problems such as hunger, poverty, and housing, which bear on the health of citizens.

Further, to justify religious belief and practice simply on the grounds that they improve one's health and lengthen one's life can convert God into a spiritual tool in the shed. Some secondary health benefits (and moral benefits) accrue from worship, but we hardly know what we are doing in worship if we worship God for that reason alone. The Supreme Being is an end in itself, not the means to some other end. Married people tend to live longer than single people. But we would question John's motives for marrying Jane if he married her on the grounds that marriage would yield him some extra months or years of life. Jane might reasonably think of herself as used rather than loved.

The love of God, rightly understood, lifts us out of the instrumental realm of "so that" and "in order to." Worship places us before the "I am that I am." To worship God "in order to" lower one's blood pressure, earn more money, catch an extra hour's sleep, or lengthen one's life confuses creaturely goods with the deity.

## The Religious Reflex before the Daunting Power of Disease and Death

A second powerful religious stream today carries forward the second shamanic myth, which interprets disease as the invasion of hostile, negative power and seeks from the healer a military counterattack. This alternative religious stream flows not out of the official religious traditions of the West, but out of a religious reflex before the dreadfulness of disease and death. Officially, the West has affirmed a God who creates, nurtures, and protects. Unofficially, however, the gods that enthrall modern men and women do not bless but threaten them. A religious preoccupation with the negative permeates modern life. It fills, for example, our mass media, which devoutly tell us of the havoc wrought by death, murder, crime, corruption, fire, panic, and tornado in the past twenty-four hours. (Newspapers might conceivably focus on events more positive—on lectures, stories of community cooperation, and biographies of inspiring people. But of course they do not, because such newspapers would not sell. Their "news" simply would not command attention. Only evil shows sufficient energy, vitality, and allure to make the headlines and command attentiveness.) In these matters, the newspapers exploit the preoccupations of the human psyche itself.

The central anxiety of modern people, argues Joseph C. Rheingold of the Harvard Medical School, is anxiety before death—not the scientist's soothing notion of a natural death, but the fear of catastrophic death, a fear that includes the dread of mutilation and abandonment.[17] The fear of bodily destruction and abandonment at the hands of the community commands the media and troubles children's dreams. Children know this double fear of death. In demanding the reassurance of a voice, the touch of a hand at bedtime, they betray that they know all the issues involved in a sleep—a burial under the cover—which gives early practice in dying. And the same death that troubles the young also threatens old people with the final collapse of their bodies and with abandonment at the hands of the community. Preoccupation with death and destructive power has largely replaced attentiveness before a good and nurturant God as the central religious experience of modern people.

In the historic religious tradition, people responded to a nurturant God in three basic ways. The faithful responded with awe before God; and sinners either fought God or fled him. Correspondingly, today we tend to respond in three basic ways to disease and death: (1) we respond to death with awe, a reflex that includes both fear and a shy, almost loving embrace of the event; but, more usually, (2) we react to death by waging an all-out fight against it; or (3) we fall into patterns of avoidance and denial. Inevitably, these three responses produce three different notions of the healer's role. Most dominantly, a religious preoccupation with destructive power today generates the parental and military strategies of modern medicine. These strategies reflect the second shamanic response to disease as negative, invasive power. The doctor and nurse emerge as protectors and fighters against its onslaught.

1. *The Healer as Parent.* Insofar as physicians respond to the patient's urge to avoid death, they tend

to become parental figures who reassure their children and shelter them from the powers that are killing them. Kindness rather than candor becomes the chief moral virtue one expects from a professional. The physician assumes the role, in effect, of the Inquisitor in Dostoevsky's legend, the role of the great humanitarian, who offers miracle, mystery, and authority: a medical miracle, wrapped up in a Latin mystery, and passed off with authority, thereby offering relief from suffering and a deferral of reckoning with death. I do not mean to mock this image of the healer. It is a powerful humanistic response to the experience of crushing power. Because in the culture at large the nurturant God appears to be dead, the professional assumes the role of protector and nurturer.

2. *The Healer as Fighter.* Alternatively, the physician looms as the fighter against death, the titan who responds to the sacred by seizing power in his or her own right and doing battle with the enemy—cancer or heart attack. Patients prize a kind of military intelligence, tactical brilliance, self-confidence, and stamina in the physician. The hero, in this case, plays the role of Dr. Rieux in Camus's *The Plague*, who compassionately and without illusions fights against destructive power. This image, of course, extends beyond medicine in the modern world. Often we highly value a fighting spirit in other professionals—the lawyer, the politician, the business executive—as they attempt to do battle in the face of heavy odds.

3. *The Healer as Companion in Death.* Finally, a small group of healers today at work in terminal cases would have their patients neither fight nor avoid death, but see death as "the saving moment." They look to death and dying for the deepening and ennobling of the human. Elisabeth Kübler-Ross, leader of the thanatol-

ogists, sees death in this way. Going through the "five stages" with Kübler-Ross becomes a way of fulfilling one's humanity, achieving a final intimacy with others and an equanimity about one's life. No one could watch the Broadway version of this *ars moriendi* (Michael Christofer's play *Shadow Box*) without realizing that the play, and the outlook it dramatized, provided a substitute religious experience for the unsynagogued and the unchurched. At its worst, this view verges on a sentimental worship of death; but at its best, as exemplified in the hospice movement, it reminds us that there are things we can do for one another even when we lose the physical battle. This newly defined role for the healer partly recovers that other task of the shaman—as undertaker, as escort and companion from the land of the living to that of the dead.

Of these three contending models for interpreting the healer, the image of the physician as parent until recently prevailed. Until fifty years ago, the physician could offer little in the fight against death. Classical writers likened the physician to the philosopher and the priest. *Medicus animarum medicus corporum.* The philosopher and the priest were to the soul what the medical doctor was to the body. But the philosopher traditionally offered the soul not a victory over the world but consolation before an unalterable fate, and the priest offered fatherly protection in a vale of tears. Analogously, the physician offered as much care and comfort as possible to the body; only rarely could he or she achieve a cure.

The image of the fighter has predominated in more recent decades. The modern doctor's authority derives chiefly from a grim negativity, that is, from the fear of suffering and death and from the retaliatory powers that modern biomedical research places at his or her disposal. This authority, of course, exposes the physician to a great risk. Patients and their families now hope to receive from the physician a victory and may turn on the latter in defeat.

## The Biblical Setting

This book not only explores each of the images in the setting of the religious reflex that gives rise to them; it also examines the alternative religious vision that the West derives from the biblical tradition. That tradition affirms the holy of holies to be creative, nurturant, and donative, rather than destructive. It does not deny the reality of disease, suffering, and death or our tremor before them but puts them in the context of a power that encompasses them. God's power ultimately prevails in the midst of disease and death. An excellent term to describe the empowering "tie" of men and women to the sacred so perceived is the biblical term "covenant." The covenant illuminates the patterns of resistance, avoidance, and worship of death and reveals that, although they differ in many ways, they still make the same metaphysical mistake: They all take death too seriously; they assume that death has the last word, that death defines, without significant remainder, the healer's task. This non-covenantal religious reflex ultimately falsifies the goals of medicine and compromises the ties between the patient and the healer.

## Chapter One

# Parent

T raditionally, the adversarial image dominated the practice of the law; the parental, the practice of medicine. The first evokes a sword; the second, a shield against trouble. The first, aggressive realism, if not cynicism; the second, benevolent and even compassionate care.

The current phrase "family physician" preserves the parental image at a time when it must contend with two other images: those of the technician and the mercenary fighter. The phrase suggests ambiguity. At one level, "family physician" means a professional who can offer primary care to all family members. The family practitioner generalizes in an age of specialization or, if one prefers, specializes in primary care.

At another level, "family physician" means not just a generalist who has learned the skills to deal with the diverse problems of all the family members, male and female, young and old, but also a professional who recognizes that illness itself can shake the whole family. When one person in a family gets sick, the whole family falls subtly ill. Illness upsets the equilibrium, the rhythm, the homeostasis, not just of the body but of the entire social unit. Thus the family physician should be resourceful not simply in dealing with diverse diseases but also in helping the whole family cope with the impact of illness. The technically oriented specialist may overlook this impact and fail to cultivate those more subtle personal skills and virtues that can help the family recover.

Traditionally—romantically—the family physician not only cared for the whole family but functioned almost as a member of the family. He cared for the parents, delivered their babies, and saw grandparents through their last illnesses. Delivering these services, he knew what it was to venture out beyond the office and hospital setting. He made house calls, drank family coffee, and savored gossip. On a home visit, his rump had to adjust to the sprung coil in the living room sofa; his eye took in the state of tidiness or disarray of the home and its keepers. He knew the personal and social setting of disease almost as intimately as any family member, and, just as important, the family knew him personally. In the language of the sociologists, the relationship to the physician was *gemeinschaftlich* rather than *gesellschaftlich*, inherited rather than chosen, familial rather than organizational.

Willa Cather offers a highly romantic version of just such a physician in her story entitled "Neighbor Rosicky," whose Doctor Ed fits into the pattern of small town and rural America. Indeed, the physician symbolizes that humane, personal care that, in the eyes of the dying farmer, establishes the moral superiority of country to city life.

> In the country, if you had a mean neighbor, you could keep off his land and keep him off yours. But in the city, all the foulness and misery and brutality of your neighbors was part of your life. . . . Here, if you were sick, you had Dr. Ed

to look after you; and if you died, fat Mr. Hay-
cock, the kindest man in the world, buried you.[1]

The traditional family physician assumed a very
particular role in family life—not that of brother, sister, or cousin, but of parent, a superparent, specifically
the father. The physician acted like a father in those
crises in which the assault of illness drove various
members of the family, adults included, to look for
respite from their responsibilities as workers, lovers,
and parents. They needed to lay down their normal
burdens and to submit to the ravages and perplexities
of disease and to the firm directions, regimen, and
drugs of the ministering professional. Sick adults
receive permission, as it were, to act childishly. Thus,
even today, a young resident in surgery, just rounding
thirty, feels free to approach, in the recovery room,
the bed of a seventy-year-old man and to call him, just
awakening from anesthesia, by his first name (not the
formal name by which the world knows him as a
worker, citizen, or stranger, but by John, Arthur, or
Bill, the name to which he answers to friends and family) and to wake him gently, as a father would summon
his child from sleep.

In traditional Western society, the father figure had
special responsibility for order; the mother, for nurture. Parental order protected the child against the
various assaults of anomie; nurture helped to
strengthen the child against crisis and its aftermath.
Both forms of parenting demand self-expenditure and
compassion, the moral marks of parenting. Without
self-expenditure and compassion, the relationship
rots. The imbalance in knowledge and power between
parent and child easily leads to exploitation unless rel-
evant parental virtues compensate for this imbalance.

The two virtues connect. Self-expenditure defines the parent chiefly as the giver, the child as the receiver. But the parent also receives from the child. Unlike philanthropists or benefactors who relate to others solely by their giving, parents receive a portion of their very meaning from the relationship. By virtue of this deep identity with their children, parents also "suffer with" them. Compassion marks the relationship. In this respect, parents also differ from philanthropists. A gulf separates the philanthropic giver from the receiver. The philanthropist may sympathize, but, qua philanthropist, he or she does not suffer with the beneficiary. Philanthropists, no matter how much they give, always give out of surplus. Their own identity is not at stake. Parental expenditure, however, is always in some degree self-expenditure.

Ordinary family life can corrupt each of these moral features of parenting. The mother and father's imposition of order turns authoritarian and repressive; their nurture sometimes produces endless dependence; their self-expenditure exacts a guilty indebtedness from their offspring; and their compassion often prevents them from offering objective and efficacious help. Uncriticized, the parental image hardly offers much aid in interpreting the physician's role. It merely sentimentalizes the older stereotypical image of the fatherly, sometimes pampering, bedside sympathizer who specialized in soothing the well-to-do.

The Western theological tradition offers some help in exploring the relevance of the parental image to medicine. For in applying the image analogically to God, the tradition had to engage in criticism of the human image. In speaking of God as parent, the tradition contrasted the ordinary human family with a divine family, spaciously ordered, nurturing, and empowering, in which self-expenditure liberates rather than burdens, and compassion does not melt into an ineffectual sympathy. If the image has any continuing relevance whatsoever to medicine, it needs to take into account some of this theological criticism.

Only subject to this criticism does it make sense to talk about the parental element in healing. First and most obviously, the physician should exhibit the moral marks of good parenting: compassion for the patient's plight and a readiness to sacrifice for his or her good. Like the parental relationship, the therapeutic presupposes a marked imbalance in knowledge and power that, if unchecked by compassion and self-giving, quickly deteriorates into rank exploitation. The healer, like the parent, primarily gives effort and knowledge for the well-being of the patient. The latter, chiefly, but not exclusively, receives. Healers, like parents, receive from the relationship their living, to be sure, and, ultimately, more than their living: their vocation, healing. Healing requires patients who lay their bodies on the line.

Furthermore, the physician, like the good parent, engages in a limited providential activity—care. Adequate health care demands knowledge of the patient's history—physical, personal, and social. Without it, the physician cannot know fully the etiology of disease, trace its course, and estimate the patient's resources. The healer must also, like a parent, provide a momentary haven against threats that beset both from without and from within. The very word "hospital" reminds us of the pilgrim's need for shelter. The bearing of the physician should invite the patient to let whatever inwardly besets come to the surface—the tics, complaints, lumps, and irregularities of the body and the dark side of the psyche. Indeed, the physician touches and probes the body and psyche, as no one other than parents may do. The physician forecasts through diagnosis and prognosis—acts that reflect the cognitive element in providence. The physician sees into the past and present in such a way as to see ahead into the future. Then, through therapeutic intervention, the physician reflects the practical side of providence by making provision against the future, however harsh it may be.

Healing, finally, reflects both paternal and maternal parenting; it provides both order and nurture. The onset of disease disrupts, disorients, and confounds body rhythms, psychological equilibrium, and work patterns. The patient needs rescue from the threat of anomie, and that person comes to live by an order and a regimen that the physician dictates for the patient's good. At the same time, disease has enfeebled the patient; help is needed to recover strength and power. These two aspects of the parental role, the ordering and the nurturant, have tended to assimilate, the one to the medical and the other to the nursing profession: The physician chiefly prescribes and orders; the nurse chiefly assists, empowers, and nurtures. But both professions, in fact, acknowledge obligations to structure and to empower the lives of those in their charge.

The parental image functions destructively in two ways: first, through the example of the bad parent; second, through the misapplication of the image. When the healer, like the good parent, self-expends, shows compassion, watches over, and provides order and nurture, well and good. But the healer overreaches when he or she justifies overriding the patient's wants, wishes, decisions, and judgment on the grounds that the adult patient is a child, incapable of knowing his or her own good. When professionals behave this way toward an adult in full possession of mental faculties, they mock the restraint of the providence of God and they distort the virtues that parenting would elicit by imposing on the patient a loss of stature and freedom. Forthwith the parental image deteriorates into paternalism (or, more broadly, parentalism).

## The Decline of the Image

Whatever its earlier attractions, defects, and structural limits, apparently the parental image no longer automatically shapes lives in either the social order at large or the medical profession in particular. Modern society has changed its basic model for interpreting social arrangements from the familial to the contractual. As late as the sixteenth century, Luther relied heavily on the parental image to explain the authority of the state.[2] He discussed the state's authority and civic duty under the heading of the Fourth Commandment—to honor one's father and mother. A paternalistic political model prevailed in Protestant, Catholic, and Eastern Orthodox areas of Europe and Asia (altogether eclipsing the classical Aristotelian image of defining the *polis* as a community of friends). Although a covenantal image emerged for interpreting community in the Netherlands and in England in the seventeenth century (more will be said about this essentially biblical image later in this book), a secular, contractualist model has increasingly shaped social thought in the modern West.

The distinction already made between *gemeinschaft* and *gesellschaft* captures the major difference between the familial and contractualist models. The first type of social organization derives community from origins (family, church, and nation); the second type bases community chiefly on shared ends (of workplace, interest groups, and free associations). The first derives largely from the fate of birth; we inherit it. The second emerges from shared goals; society chooses it. The first orients to the past; it relishes permanence. The second orients to the future; it adapts to the contingent.

The familial type of social arrangement thrives on the familiar; the contractual gears itself to deal with the novel. The modern world increasingly reflects the contractualist understanding of social organization, so much so that the state itself claims to derive from a primordial social contract; religion appears a matter of choice, to say nothing of marriage, university education, workplace, and the marketplace choice of a doctor. Even though institutions that serve ends, such as the corporation, the labor union, and the professional association, gradually take on the characteristics of a *gemeinschaft*, offering familial satisfactions to those who participate in their life, a marketplace contractualism increasingly dominates modern Western life.

The very transience of modern life tends to render the parental image obsolete and to encourage contractualism. *Gemeinschaftlich* community, especially, requires some measure of stability and continuity. People who move, on the average, once every five years find it increasingly difficult to rely on relations inherited rather than chosen. Most Americans, sooner or later, choose a new doctor in a new town or go to a clinic or emergency room to see interchangeable doctors. Physicians and patients meet as strangers. They agree to exchange services for money; they do not face a crisis as surrogate family members.

The medical profession reflects this general trend toward contractualism in its delivering of care and medical education. The bureaucratization and specialization of medicine today mean that no one person, not even a family practitioner, ministers to the whole family or even to the whole person. The notion of providential activity that underlies analogically the vocation of the parent and that defines, in turn, the diagnostic, prognostic, and therapeutic work of the physician presupposes a unitary, directoral intelligence that now fragments in a bureaucratic setting.

Changes in medical education have also contributed to the eclipse of the parental image. Historically, the parental image defined not simply the physician's relationship to patients but also—and even more intensively—the relationship of the senior physician-mentor to his junior colleagues or colleagues-to-be. In the Hippocratic tradition, the young physician-to-be actually looked on his teacher as his adoptive father and, in gratitude for training, accepted some filial obligations toward him and his family. This tradition continued through the apprenticeship system, into the twentieth century; vestigial remains of familial obligation show up in modern notions of professional courtesy.

But medical education has shifted increasingly out of a personal, familial ambience into the impersonal, highly competitive, technical, and meritocratic setting of the modern university and its teaching hospital. This change in educational atmosphere powerfully affects the young physician's view of patients. A wise physician, when asked once how one teaches compassion to young professionals, remarked that the teacher must, first of all, deal compassionately with students. In his *Cancer Ward*, Alexander Solzhenitsyn offers an impressive maternal image for the physician in Ludmila Afanasyevna, a senior physician on the hospital staff. More than coincidentally, however, her junior staff members—not her patients—call her "mother."[3] She communicates her nurturant qualities effectively in the work of the institution partly because she relates this way not only to patients but also to her own staff.

Conversely, young students who have not enjoyed parental sanctuary in the course of their professional education are unlikely to know how to offer it to patients. Indeed, having lived themselves in fear of failure and won their own place in the world through hard-driving ambition, they look on their patients as biological failures, broken-down machines that one disdainfully patches up.

## The Image Persists

Despite appearances to the contrary, the parental image persists even under the conditions of a huge, impersonal, anonymous mass society (that delivers health care largely to strangers and often in the context of total institutions). But it persists in a modified and subtly amplified form. Professionals continue to diminish the patient's freedom for the patient's benefit, but not usually in a small-scale, intimate, familial setting.

Managerialism or puppeteerism more aptly describes the professional mode and the patient's plight. Patients experience less the overbearing presence of a mother or a father than a behind-the-scenes management of their lives. The phrases "patient management," "grief management," and "management of the terminally ill" reflect the behavior pattern in which we save the vices and throw out some of the virtues of the parental image.

Impersonal manipulation differs from traditional paternalism at two points. First, managers, unlike mothers or fathers, veil feeling. Authority achieves impersonality. The patient submits to technical—rational, rather than personal—controls. The controller's face fades; it becomes more elusive; but the controller's power is no less real. Second, managers seek to control not only a patient's behavior but his or her feelings. They anticipate and then loop within the circle of their control the patient's "emotional" responses.[4] Professionals thereby resemble less the traditional parent who barks out commands—"Stop that" or "Shut up!"—and more the liberal parent of the 1950s onward who is inclined to say, "We don't like to do that, do we?" (This liberal parental style itself may well reflect and mimic prevailing forms of managerial authority.)

The traditional style seems more overtly authoritarian, but, in fact, it restricts the scope of its authority to behavior: It leaves the child free to feel as he or she pleases—as long as the child curbs the prohibited behavior. The traditional parent demanded external compliance, but not the child's soul. The liberal seems more polite, perhaps even more deferential to the child's feelings, but, in fact, presumes to know and, at length, even to steer interior responses.

The health care professions have created today a generation of managers who have made themselves experts in the stages of dying (denial, anger, bargaining, resignation, and hope), grieving, growing up, divorcing, giving birth to the retarded, and adjusting to trauma, accident, and burn. The literature assumes a transparent and malleable patient—not only in behavior but in attitude and spirit.

This managerial authority produces the total institution: so named not only because activities normally distributed across a number of sites (working, sleeping, eating, and socializing) take place in a single setting but also because the residents of the institution tend to belong to the institution totally—in interior life as well as outer behavior.

Only a small number of physicians practice in total institutions, but a large percentage of young residents train in inner-city hospitals. There they see a stream of patients, battered, distraught, uneducated, often resourceless, who only too willingly yield to them parental authority. "That's OK, Doc, whatever you say. Fine. Just take care of it. I want it taken care of." The young physician quickly assimilates and generalizes from this early experience to his or her subsequent practice. The physician has said too many times, "Well, Mr. Jones, before we let you go, there are some tests we have to do," and has discovered that the patient asks no questions. The patient does not know, or want to know, what the tests are for, and within minutes he phones his wife, "They've got a few more tests they have to run before I can get out of here." In a technical sense, these often-repeated transactions are not instances of paternalism. Patients actively thrust parental authority on the physician. Formally, the physician has not deprived the patient of freedom. But once playing the parent, the physician finds manipulating or circumventing the will or wishes of the balky patient easy and natural. Thus the surgeon tells the patient afraid of an operation: "If you don't have it, your blood will poison, your leg will rot, and you will die." But the patient's fear also prompts the surgeon not to explain in understandable detail the procedure's risk of infection and hemorrhage. As one hematologist-oncologist put it, "There are informed consent papers, to be sure, but at the same time you should know I can talk a patient into anything."

## The Antipaternalists

Philosophers from John Stuart Mill forward have pressed the attack against paternalism and offered in the course of that attack a useful definition of formally paternalistic behavior. In his essay *On Liberty*, Mill stated: "Neither one person, nor any number of persons, is warranted in saying to another human creature of ripe years, that he not do with his life for his own benefit what he chooses to do with it."[5] The paternalist or parentalist interferes with (or circumvents) the liberty, autonomy, wishes, or judgment of another adult but justifies this behavior on the ground of the latter's benefit. Such interference, in effect, reduces an adult to a child, albeit for the child's own sake. This definition excludes a second and a third type of imposition on others. In the second case, one limits the actions of others to protect third parties (e.g., physicians who report cases of social disease to public authority). In the third instance, one restricts the freedom of others for one's own convenience or advantage (e.g., one tamps down inmates with drugs to make them more manageable). A given intervention, of course, may appeal to all three reasons for interfering with the wants and wishes of another, in which case the parentalism is "impure" (e.g., a physician administers a drug that a patient, if free to choose, might have opposed, but the physician expects that through the treatment the patient will function better in the pursuit of his or her own goals and will disrupt less the caretakers and others as well). In cases of pure professional parentalism, however, the caretaker, acting on the basis of superior knowledge and power, circumvents the patient for the latter's benefit alone.

Mill directed his fire chiefly against paternalism in politics. During the nineteenth and twentieth centuries, social reformers extended the criticism to the paternalistic policies of company towns and total institutions. Conservatives and radicals alike in the 1970s attacked what they saw as the paternalism of the welfare state. Philosophers and theologians, at work in biomedical ethics, have done elegant work on the subject primarily as the problem impinges on the subject of informed consent.

The mass media, through plays, movies, and television dramas, have focused the challenge on all those persons, professionals included, who would reduce, even for the most benevolent of reasons, an adult to the charge or property of another. We consider two works of art of unequal merit that exemplify paternalism. The first conveniently lays out the antipaternalist argument as the popular understanding perceives it, and the second places the argument in the context of its often-unacknowledged religious setting.

## Whose Life Is It Anyway?

The hero and protagonist of Brian Clark's play *Whose Life Is It Anyway?* puts this question in his relentless attack against paternalism. Ken Harrison lies immobile but highly verbal at center stage—six months deep into his life in an institution. A talented sculptor, he broke his neck in a traffic accident and lost the use of all his body but his head. Chief among his deprivations, he can no longer sculpt or make love. His chief complaint is directed at the medical staff that prolongs—against his will—his already impoverished life.

Enough time has passed since the accident both to make clear the limits of his recovery (he will be paralyzed for life) and to carry him beyond the trauma-induced depression. Indeed, he shows great wit and charm; his nurses, physicians, and the audience find him utterly appealing. He has decided, however, to escape this plight by discharge from the hospital, knowing that, once removed from its support system, he will die in six days.

The chief consultant and paternalist in the case, Dr. Emerson, opposes his plan. He interprets the request for dismissal as proof of Harrison's depression and orders him forcibly tranquilized. The patient challenges the physician's right to tranquilize him on the grounds that the doctor is doing it for his own benefit, not Harrison's. "You . . . watched me disturbed, worried . . . and you can't do anything for me—nothing that really matters. I'm paralyzed and you're impotent. This disturbs you. . . . So I get the tablet and you get the tranquillity."[6] The episode of the tranquilizer, strictly speaking, does not pose the issue of parentalistic behavior. Parents show bad faith if they pretend to intervene for the child's benefit but actually manipulate the child for their own sake. Superordinates exploit when they intervene, for their own sake, in the life of the subordinate against the latter's wishes. Furthermore, they deceive when they pretend that something other than self-protection impels them. The episode of the tranquilizer unmasks: The physician behaves in this instance like a false parent who uses his children to serve himself.

But the main thrust of the play strikes against paternalism and, specifically, that demeaning notion of a parent-child relationship that presupposes the child as property. The doctor's use of the possessive "my" in "my patient" becomes a statement about ownership. (I *have* an MI in Room 453, a quadriplegic on the next corridor.) The patient retaliates in the language of property. (My life belongs to me and to me alone. I have absolute disposition over my own life. It is not my doctor's, not my parents', and not my fiancée's. I can do with it as I please.)

Thus the play dramatizes the central issue: patient autonomy versus paternalistic authority. The title of the play leaves no doubt about where the playwright stands, and audiences have left little doubt about where upper-middle-class culture stands. The audience quickly lines up with the hero against the medical establishment—against both the determined Dr. Emerson, who would force Harrison to stay alive, and the social worker, who would hook him up to reading machines and comptometers to improve his quality of life.

The conclusion does not surprise. Harrison persuades a lawyer to press his case in a court inquiry held at his bedside. The judge decides in his favor. The audience applauds. The defeated doctor graciously offers to let him stay in the hospital without life support systems but still hopes that before he lapses into a coma Harrison will change his mind.

Long before Tom Conti dazzled audiences in London and New York with his performance as the patient, the drama had succeeded as an audiovisual tape on the medical ethics circuit. I first saw it back in 1972. Since its Broadway run, it has transmuted itself into a movie. For all its success, the play is shallow.

The play poses only the legal question of whether Ken Harrison can discharge himself from the hospital to die. It systematically ignores the *moral* question: Should he do it? I say "systematically" because the playwright manipulates the story to keep the moral question from surfacing. He gives the patient a social environment composed exclusively of professional nurses, doctors, a social worker, lawyers. That limitation, of course, is not entirely arbitrary. Catastrophe often converts one's social world from the personal and familial to the professional. But Clark effectively eliminates from the drama those persons whose intimate ties to the patient would raise the question of whether he ought to kill himself.

The playwright conveniently avoids the moral complication that Harrison's fiancée and his mother would have introduced. Harrison had dismissed his fiancée two weeks before the drama begins on the grounds that "she's a young healthy woman. She wants babies—real ones. Not ones that never *will* learn to walk."[7] And he reports that his Scottish mother acceded to his wishes with the comment, "Aye, lad, it's thy life: Don't worry about your dad— I'll get him over it."[8] Having conveniently dispatched offstage the girlfriend and the family, Clark can turn to the hospital staff, whose role is *only* professional, seasoned with a dash of transient sentiment. Staff members are close enough to Harrison to make his death poignant but not so close as to suffer deeply. This emotional distance is just about where the audience is located. From their privileged shelter, they can get behind the banner of autonomy without raising too many questions about its right uses.

To put the same point dramatically rather than morally, the play does not pit a protagonist against a serious antagonist. (The doctor hardly counts as a worthy opponent. Legally, the patient can discharge himself from the hospital. He is resoundingly sane.) Only the patient's own wit and charm provide an antagonist. Members of the audience hope he wins his duel with the doctor; they applaud his final legal triumph. But then their applause trails off. They suddenly realize that his winning means they lose this appealing man. His charm provides the only undertow to his vigorously pressed pursuit of the freedom to die. Thus the play closes with Ken Harrison alone on the stage: a charming man without ties and therefore apparently without any serious moral struggle.

This antipaternalist play blurts out some of the moral limits of antipaternalism. Clearly, the paternalist demeans the patient when he or she rides roughshod over the patient's formal and legally sanctioned liberty. But in subtle ways, the antipaternalist also diminishes the patient. Patients tend to shrink morally if they proclaim no more than the indeterminate liberty over which they preside while caring not a fig about how they act. In the libertarian perspective, it suffices simply that patients make *their own decisions*. *What* decisions they make or what behavior they display is not of interest—beyond minimal concerns that they do not interfere with the similar liberty of others. Liberty diminishes to negative liberty alone: freedom from, not freedom for. This apparent respect for autonomy actually consigns the patient to moral oblivion. If we do not bother to judge actions, we imply that neither the act nor the actor matters.

In one of the subtler exchanges in the play, Clark touches momentarily on this problem. Ken Harrison criticizes the social worker for failing to reprimand him for his own bad behavior. Harrison rightly interprets her condescending tolerance as the worst sort of exclusion. Deviant or stricken groups (patients, criminals, elderly people) take a first step back into community when others treat them as more than mere bundles of morally indifferent wants and interests. Paternalists fail to respect others when they preempt their negative liberty, but only too often antipaternalists fail to respect others when they patronize any and all forms of its exercise.

In its usual expressions, antipaternalism also diminishes the professional's moral responsibility. Antipaternalism rightly indicts the physician who intervenes officiously in the lives of others, either for the professional's own sake (I get the Valium, and you get the tranquillity) or for the sake of the patient (It's my unconditional obligation to save your life). But antipaternalism tends to overlook those additional professional responsibilities above and beyond respect for liberty. It deals only with the sins of excess, not of defect. Patients marked by liberty alone, without moral responsibility, can expect only technical services from professionals, no more. Radical antipaternalists today rail exclusively against the overbearing professional, but professionals are increasingly "underbearing" rather than overbearing. In the commercial world of today, antipaternalism often combines with libertarian assumptions to produce a callous, minimalist ethic.[9] The bare negatives—"Do no harm," "Do no wrong," and "Respect autonomy"—fall short of the professional's positive obligations to serve the patient's well-being.

Some philosophers today have limited their antipaternalism by adopting a so-called soft or weak paternalism.[10] They generally oppose paternalistic interventions but concede two conditions that justify such interventions: (1) when the patient already suffers from impaired autonomy either permanently (as in the case of some retarded or deranged patients) or temporarily (as in the case of those accident victims whose injuries make them momentarily incapable of deciding on their own behalf); (2) when the practitioner imposes only trivial deprivations, the least restrictive possible in scope or duration (for example, when the physician chooses among equally effective drug regimens the alternative that imposes the least deprivation or dependence). In taking these conditions seriously, the physician concedes, in effect, that the burden of proof rests on the physician to justify the intervention, rather than on the patient to justify rejection of the treatment.

Theoretically, an intervention justified by the first of these conditions (already impaired autonomy) does not qualify as paternalistic in that the doctor cannot deprive a patient of autonomy if the patient does not enjoy it in the first place. One cannot deprive a child of adulthood. Practically, however, the claim of impaired autonomy opens a sliding door through which much well and not so well intentioned action can squeeze. Impaired autonomy obviously includes severe cases of mental retardation, emotional disturbance, or catastrophic suspensions of rational power. More subtly, it covers borderline impairments of will resulting from pressures (external or emotional) that the patient may find it hard to resist without intervention. It also includes deficits in knowledge that prevent a patient from appreciating the evils that the intervention precludes. A particularly exalted definition of a truly autonomous act allows more and more second-party interventions in the name of impaired capacity. This criterion moves professionals even further in the direction of paternalism when practitioners use a patient's opposition to a procedure to prove his or her impaired capacity—just as parents often cite the rejection of their authority as evidence of a child's immaturity. *Whose Life Is It Anyway?* builds just this sort of loop when the physician interprets Ken Harrison's request for dismissal from the hospital as evidence of his post-trauma depression. In the hands of practitioners, therefore, this modified antipaternalism can increase paternalism by shifting the burden of proof from the physician and forcing the patient to prove his or her competence.

A third way of justifying a paternalistic intervention appeals not to the patient's incompetence or to the triviality of the imposed deprivation but to the enormity of the evil that the patient would suffer apart from the intrusion. Those who shift to this third criterion accept the assumptions of a "strong" rather than a "weak" paternalist. They justify burdensome interventions, irrespective of the patient's formal competence, if the evils from which they preserve the patient seem irreversible, dangerous, and all-encompassing. Dr. Emerson, who would preserve the sculptor from the irreversible evil of death, exemplifies this approach. From Ken Harrison's perspective, however, the deprivation from which he will suffer at the hands of the physician exceeds death itself; he will lose the freedom to escape his radically impoverished life. Given this impasse, the determination of competence becomes decisive not only in this play but in much of the literature on paternalism.

The third way of justifying paternalism—by invoking the evils that the intervention prevents—deserves more attention than either the play or recent philosophical literature gives it. Otherwise, one fails to deal with the dangerous side of parentalism—both its tragic dignity and its moral and religious appeal. One fails, in brief, to understand why conscientious parents crush their children in the very effort to nurture and preserve them.

## The Legend of the Grand Inquisitor

Dostoevsky offers the best insight into the somber glory and religious depth of parentalism in the great soliloquy of the Inquisitor in *The Brothers Karamazov*. The story describes a figure much more universal than either a church inquisitor or an authoritarian socialist. The Inquisitor articulates the deepest convictions of the archhumanitarian. He urgently loves humankind. The Inquisitor wants, above all else, to protect people from suffering. He wants their happiness. Two realities determine the Inquisitor: his passionate love for human beings and the grim evils from which he desires to protect them. No other factor enters the equation; no other power, transcendent or otherwise, could possibly act in and through human suffering. The absence of any such power is the Grand Inquisitor's secret, the great burden he and those like him bear on behalf of the happiness of humankind.

The Grand Inquisitor (through the mouth of Ivan Karamazov) speaks:

> And all will be happy, all the millions of creatures except the hundred thousand who rule over them. For only we, who guard the mystery, shall be unhappy. There will be thousands of millions of happy babes, and a hundred thousand sufferers who have taken upon themselves the curse of the knowledge of good and evil. Peacefully they will die . . . and beyond the grave they will find nothing but death.[11]

Ivan's brother Alyosha, who listens attentively, breaks in on the story and exclaims about the likes of the Inquisitor:

Your Inquisitor does not believe in God, that's his secret.[12]

Alyosha's accusation of atheism does not imply that the Inquisitor lacks piety or religious devotion. He is profoundly religious. He does not, however, worship the traditional God of the Christians and Jews. Destructive power, not life, awes him: what James Joyce later called in *Ulysses* "*Dio Boia*," the "hangman god." The Inquisitor compassionately seeks to protect his charges from suffering and death. Death, so interpreted, does not dwindle to the biological incident that ends human life. It appears and expands through all those destructive forces that grip the heart with love, fear, hope, worry, and flight, long before the end arrives, whenever the concert ends, the meal grows cold, or the career turns barren in one's hands.

The power that brings death besets men and women on every side. It stampedes them from behind into frenetic activities—as they pursue a career, virtuosity, or the display of some glory, hoping to escape their metaphysical solitude by outlining themselves against a dark background. It attacks them frontally as they mount their battles against their threatening enemies, whether soldiers, competitors, or siblings. It ambushes from the side—the young, the high-minded, the hedonists, and the frivolous—with the unexpectedness of a clipping in a football game. It stirs beneath human life in the profoundest of pleasures, as it touches with melancholy the marriage bed or as it burdens with guilt the encounters between the generations. And at night, it settles down from above and breathes gently in old men and women who, weary of all other forms of fleeing, fighting, and sidestepping death, long now for sleep.

The Inquisitor, in effect, sees all that; he tragically understands those powers that environ us. He knows that his charges will find nothing beyond the grave. They belong eventually to death. And thus, on this side of the grave, given his overwhelming love, he wants to protect them. He seeks to offer them what Melville calls in *Moby Dick* the "Isle of Safety." The archetypal mother-father, he wants to create and provide for the human family, to establish a temporary sanctuary. He knows that this Isle of Safety contradicts the organizing principle of the universe, but he seeks in its confines to found a tolerable degree of warmth, intimacy, and order—until the earth shakes, the tide rolls in, and the winds blow. In this temporary shelter, the ruling principle, the *avoidance* of suffering and death, governs every action. Therefore he must send the silent but disturbing stranger (Christ) on his way. He cannot suffer the presence of Christ, whose life would open up men and women to that dreadful knowledge and consequent freedom that blaspheme the Grand Inquisitor's religion.

The Inquisitor resembles and works for the Antichrist—not the trivial, villainous figure of popular piety, but the great cosmic figure who parodies the Christ. Like the Christ, the Inquisitor loves humankind; like the Christ, he suffers dreadful isolation from his fellows; like the Christ, he sacrifices for his fellows. The parental image in the narrative fairly cries out. The Inquisitor acknowledges two kinds of people—those who lucidly understand the human condition and those who, like children, do not. In protecting his wards from the truth, the Inquisitor accepts his isolation from the human race. His knowledge deprives him of happiness, and his love deprives him of friends. Lucidly knowing his own condition, he deceives others about theirs and thereby reduces them wholly to the status of children for the sake of their happiness.

The modern conscientious parent occupies a religious position similar to that of the Grand Inquisitor. Conscientious parents envisage only two realities in the world: their love for their children and the suffering from which they want to save them. They worry about all those catastrophic possibilities that lie ahead for their children—a Mack truck bearing down the highway, a skidding motorcycle, bad grades, a mediocre college, a disastrous love affair, a rudderless career, a bad marriage, and middle-aged ennui. As conscientious parents, they cannot believe that the decisive powers in the universe could possibly do anything worthwhile in and through the suffering of their children. They alone bear the burden of succor and counsel. They take on themselves the responsibilities of a father-mother savior; and, of course, because they cannot do a very good job as saviors, they are filled with apprehension. What an anomaly it must be for children to see their parents attend a church or synagogue and yet betray, by the worry written across their faces, their great secret fear that God is dead!

In one respect, the parents wield power more ambiguously than the Inquisitor. Because they know about the human condition, they do not want their children to know too soon, and, because the parents half-know, they themselves do not want to know too much. Like the Inquisitor, they deceive, but, unlike the Inquisitor, they also seek to self-deceive. They not only create the Isle of Safety for their children; they also try to live in it themselves. Their behavior betrays an unstable mix of awareness and avoidance. Given this ambivalence, the parents, when they themselves must face pain and death, look for someone who will serve them in turn as Grand Inquisitor.

The physician assumes the same role toward the patient and his or her family that parents originally assumed toward their children, except, if anything, more intensively so. The physician faces a family in immediate crisis, whereas the parents faced the diffuse vulnerability of the child. The physician assumes the role of the humanitarian, equipped, as we have seen, with the three resources of the Inquisitor: miracle, mystery, and authority. The family looks to the physician for a medical miracle wrapped up in a Latin mystery and accompanied by authoritative instructions on how to behave, so that "everything may be done that has to be done." Once again, the doctor invokes as moral justification for the enterprise the same argument the Inquisitor used—the relief of suffering and the deferral of reckoning with death. The physician tries to deal with those powers that command the universe for the sake of the happiness of his or her charges.

Put another way, parentalism in medicine keenly experiences the absence of divine providence and substitutes a providence of its own. But it redefines providence. The providence it offers does not reckon with the turmoil of freedom within and the pain of suffering without. In order to protect its charges, this substitute providence withholds knowledge, circumvents freedom, and avoids coping with death. It exercises a tight control. Thus the patient shrinks into the physician's property, in rebuttal to which the patient can only claim that he owns him- or herself.

The Eastern Orthodox religious tradition on which Dostoevsky drew offers an alternative to the parentalist strategy. This alternative stands out most clearly in the sacrament of infant Baptism and in the activity of intercessory prayer. Divested of all its conventional sentiment, the sacrament of Baptism boldly asks parents who, above all others, want to believe that they own another human being—abjectly dependent on them, weak and needy—to hand over this tempting property into the hands of another. The sacrament insists, at the very beginning of all the feeding, sheltering, diapering, consoling, advising, financing, and rebuking that parents will indulge in across a span of twenty to thirty years, that their child does not belong to them; it belongs to another, and not just to any other, but to another who in the language of the creed "suffered under Pontius Pilate, was crucified, dead, and buried." The sacrament insists that deity does not withdraw—either from death or from the whole arena of conflict, suffering, and dying. Quite the contrary, new life comes solely through an act in which the Savior lays down his life, and believers acknowledge in Baptism their participation in this event. Thus Baptism breaks with the language of property that informs all parentalism, or, rather, it reintroduces the language at a deeper, revolutionary level. Owners discover that another wholly owns them and their children.

In the religious life, the prayers of intercession carry forward this altered sense of responsibility. Those who pray normally offer the intercessions of the heart on behalf of those whom they love or over whom they exercise some responsibility and control. Conscientious caretakers, especially, take themselves too seriously and fancy themselves as indispensable to those in their charge: children, patients, students, and others. To the degree to which such caretakers have a religious life, they may be further inclined to convert intercession into a cosmic extension of the petitioner's hands. God trivializes into the pharmacopoeia above, the great scalpel in the sky.

Intercessory prayer, properly understood, invites petitioners to hand their charges over into the hands of God, in the confidence that God will deal mercifully with his creatures and that, because this is the case, he will not restrict his dealings to the limits of the petitioner's fears and desires. Such intercessory prayer has immediate moral corollaries for the Christian parent and for all bearing heavy responsibility for others. The petitioners must relinquish an anxious control over those for whom they pray. To pray seriously for another is to take oneself a little less seriously. This new self-estimate opens up the possibility of a positive care and cherishing of others that no longer substitutes for an absent God. Morally, intercession invites a carefree care for others in professional life. The pretensions of Atlas may be set aside. The Inquisitor has lost his sober face.

A fourth and final dispute separates the paternalists and the antipaternalists. Paternalists justify their interventions by appealing to the patient's relative incompetence, the minimal nature of the deprivation to which the patient is subjected, and the great evil from which he or she will be protected—but also by appealing to the positive goods to which the paternalistic intervention will lead.

Oftentimes, therapists justify their action without overtly denying the patient's competence. They simply feel that they can secure the good in question more efficiently, more economically, with less wasteful investment of time, if they go directly after the good without detouring through the patient as collaborator in the enterprise. Harassed administrators—whether federal, corporate, or professional—have often guarded their power, not out of contempt for others, but because they know that persuasion and collaboration take inordinate time. That argument from efficiency works in some cases where a clear-cut consensus about goals exists and where the administrator-professional enjoys a clear-cut authority as agent for others in the pursuit of those goals. But, notoriously, those in power tend to overestimate that consensus and take for granted that authority.

Furthermore, as Daniel Brock has observed, "some states of affairs are good for a person only if he wants them."[13] Brock's comment does not imply subjectivism or relativism. He does not say that the goodness of a good depends solely on the preferences and wants of subjects. A good may be objectively a good but of a specific kind that requires the subject to participate in its production. A father may obtain a good grade for his daughter by writing a paper for her, but that intervention will not provide her with the writing skills that come only with her experience of wrestling with the paper. That good never results if the paternalistic father supplants or bypasses his child. A physician may cure some illnesses with minimum patient participation. But the "good" of preventive medicine requires that the patient actively reconstruct his or her habits of eating, sleeping, and exercise. Paternalists cannot reach certain kinds of goods. Indeed, if the paternalist crudely tries to force them on the patient, it quickly becomes apparent that the patient will resist with a kind of spiritual lockjaw. Clenched teeth usually worked against castor oil or anything else forced down one's throat "for one's own good."

Although paternalists fail to promote the patient's good when they override or bypass the patient's autonomy, antipaternalists also fail to serve that good if they minimally respect the patient as decision maker, but attend to little else. Antipaternalism often deteriorates in the hands of careerists into a minimalist ethic that serves up technical services in a crisis but does not really interest itself in the patient's long-range flourishing. Autonomists fail to serve the patient's good if they do not engage in the hard work required to assist the patient in making better decisions and developing the habits of good health. The overbearing paternalist hardly qualifies as the moral ideal, but neither does the take-it-or-leave-it dispenser of technical services. Informing the patient, persuading the patient, and helping the patient to live with the consequences of disturbing information take time and patience, and sometimes even the persistent love of a parent. We should not so distrust the parental image as to ignore the lesson it teaches us about professional responsibility. The image has its serious shortcomings, but it still signals the need for a compassionate, sometimes sacrificial, authoritative, and nurturant devotion to another's good.

*Chapter Two*

# Fighter

I n the full manifold of the plays, novels, and philosophical essays of Albert Camus, the hero defines
his life wholly by resisting death: The political rebel,
the artist, and the medical doctor heroically protest
against a world beset by destructive power. "The
order of the world is shaped by death," observes the
hero of *The Plague*.[1] In this vision of things, we cannot
reduce death to a natural, biological event; quite the
contrary, death looms as supremely antihuman, the
absolute, invincible enemy, which, nonetheless, we
must resist to affirm our humanity. In the fashion of
his time, Camus rooted this resistance in what he
called the absurdist experience (an irreconcilable conflict between the human demand for life and rational-
ity and a world that disappoints this demand through
meaningless death). His own untimely death in a
highway accident symbolized his sense of the human
condition; his literary corpus unrelentingly protested
against that condition—without illusions, however, as
to the ultimate success of that protest.

Camus, of course, was more interested in politics
than medicine. He used the metaphor of medicine in
*The Plague* to comment on the pestilence of Nazism
and the moral warrants for the resistance movement

on behalf of its victims. But the metaphor also runs in the opposite direction toward the general human plight and the medical response. Metaphysically, men and women are in the grip of destructive power. However much the pleasures of sun, beach, and bed attract them, death, in the end, does them in. Universal and democratic, death admits of no escape; it threatens to overtake us at any time. Like fighters in a resistance movement, the medical team battles as best it can, winning only skirmishes but affirming thereby a defiant attachment to life.

Camus obviously did not invent the military metaphor for the medical profession. It pervades ordinary perceptions and speech. The metaphor of war dominates the modern, popular understanding of disease and determines in countless ways the medical response. We see germs, viruses, bacteria, and cancers as invaders that break the territorial integrity of the body; they seize bridgeheads and, like an occupying army, threaten to spread, dominate, and destroy the whole. Like war, disease seems episodic; it "breaks out," it overtakes us. One can take precautions, but one never knows when it may strike; thus it edges with menace the course of life, a little like the nuclear threat that hangs over an uneasy "peace." At a remote theoretical level, we know that wars and cancers spring from causes long in the making and that, at least in principle, they should submit to rational control. But in practice, our language betrays passivity and helplessness before either kind of catastrophe. War erupts; an epidemic strikes. In either case, the afflicted suffer rather than act in the face of arbitrary, destructive power.

The human response to disease similarly conforms to the military model. Victims look for help to professionals, who, acquainted with the weapons of war, can take charge of the defense. The professional needs, first of all, "intelligence." And so medicine has developed diagnostic procedures, scanning devices, and early warning systems more complex than the radar equipment of World War II, to let the professional know the enemy's location and the scale of the attack. Furthermore, the language of war describes the mounting counterattack. We refer to the armamentarium of drugs, the bombardment of tumors with radioactive substances, to say nothing of wielding the handheld weaponry of burning iron and knife.

The spectacular success of modern medical technology has reinforced the definition of the physician as fighter. It creates a cultural momentum; it produces a moral scheme out of the technologist's impulse: What can be done should be done. The old piety toward nature yields to a new piety toward the machine. In the Middle Ages, respect for the natural impulse of self-preservation led to the prohibition against suicide; in recent times, a piety toward the machine argues for the endless prolongation of life. The sheer existence of the machinery and a team that knows how to use it argues for its mechanical employment. The machine becomes autonomous. Instead of the machine serving the patient's life and assisting that person's recovery so as to permit him or her once again to serve others, the patient serves the machine. The patient becomes a demonstration of the potency of the machine and the virtuosity of the medical team. As one resident put it: "As a university teaching service we attempt resuscitation on all patients, particularly at the beginning of the semester."[2]

As in war, the very weapons used to fight the enemy can themselves endanger those on whose behalf we wield them. We call the result of damaging a body to save it "iatrogenic illness." Radiation therapy lays waste to healthy and sick tissue alike. Drugs have untoward side effects, from bothersome to lethal, from immediate to long delayed. Many years later, some of them may kill the "cured," as a mine seeded in a harbor in wartime may, decades later, blow an unsuspecting ship out of the water. This destructiveness that the weapons themselves exude demands that we yield total control to the professional who knows how to use them—"under doctor's orders only."

The hospital becomes a military compound. It acquires something of the hallowed-grisly status of a battleground. A kind of military discipline prevails there. Assistants are orderlies. Nurses tend to become extensions of the physician's hand. The emergency room of the big-city hospital on Saturday night smacks of the wartime field hospital. Perhaps for good historical reasons, the health care team in the tertiary-care setting resembles the military organization. Its keen sense of hierarchy and protocol partly reflects the rapid expansion of the fields of specialization in medicine during World War II. Pioneers and leaders in those specialities acquired their education and/or their clinical training in military service. Thoughtful physicians have observed that this special educational ethos may have helped give a military cast to the whole enterprise—taut, hierarchical, and somewhat expedient toward expense because, of course, the battle must be won. Economy cannot substitute for victory.

Modern medicine has tended to interpret itself not only through the prism of war but through the medium of its modern practice, that is, unlimited, unconditional war. Before the twentieth century, the West, by and large, subscribed to the notion of a just war. A just war, no matter how just its cause, had to offer some prospect of victory. Further, a just war required a careful limitation of the means used to fight it. The means must discriminate (the means must respect the distinction between combatants and noncombatants) and fit proportionally to ends (the evils of the battle must not exceed the good of the outcome). But in the twentieth century, the democracies, as well as the totalitarian states, waged total, unconditional war with the commitment of all means, extraordinary as well as ordinary, to the victory. Just so, hospitals and the physician-fighter wage unconditional battle against death. At their worst, and before the advent of federal regulations, a few professionals used unconsenting patients in research protocols in the name of the general war against disease, even though no visible benefits would come to the patients in question. And at their most zealous, they sometimes subjected patients to the ordeal of battle without any hope of victory, a strategy that we have later come to define as medical futility.

Apologists for medicine have also regularly invoked the metaphor of war to generate financial support for the medical enterprise. Thereby they have funded clinical practice and basic research. Although many professions today have grown increasingly belligerent in their rhetoric, none has succeeded like medicine in securing public support on military terms; thus it presses the war on cancer and the fight against heart disease. The growth of the health care budget from 4 percent to over 14 percent of the total gross national product from 1940 to 2000 suggests that medicine indeed has become the moral equivalent of war in our time.[3]

Medical research at the beginning of the twenty-first century has pressed forward on a number of battle-fronts, none more dramatic than the field of genetics.

Progress in genetics has expanded—or at least promised to expand—the human mastery of disease and death. As a first step, genetic screening and counseling created some room for patients to maneuver, especially those making reproductive decisions. The gargantuan human genome project in the 1990s undertook the task of identifying the position of every one of the 50,000–100,000 genes in the human body. The project promises to expand the human capacity to diagnose and perhaps eventually to modify, where appropriate, any of these genes. Genetic engineering will likely expand our capacity to treat the diseases of those who die prematurely, enhance human capabilities, and extend human life beyond its current natural limits. Furthermore, germ-line or reproductive (as opposed to somatic) cell gene therapy holds out the prospect of not simply fighting disease in actual human bodies but of altering directly reproductive cells so as to prevent the transmission of the offending disease to offspring. This preemptive attack on disease through germ-line therapy dazzles the imagination and whets the appetite for investments in research, both public and private.

Various problems accompany these technological advances in the fight against disease and death. Controversies about abortion reappear in genetic screening and counseling. The problem of sealing off medical records from insurance companies and employers intensifies as genetic screening and genome mapping yield more and more diagnostic and prognostic information about patients. Although genetic engineering to prevent premature death stirs little opposition (except worries about cost), engineering to enhance human capacities (athletic prowess, IQ, temperament) or to extend life expectancy to 120 years or more raises a host of questions, demographic, social, economic, and political, as society attempts to balance the value of longevity against other fundamental human goods. Worries about unintended harms beset germ-line therapy because future generations could suffer, perhaps irreversibly, from the consequences of faulty interventions. The myth of Icarus recounts as much a tragedy for Daedalus, Icarus's father, as for the son. Daedalus fashioned the wings that allowed for his son's escape from one evil only to prepare for the son's eventual undoing. Germ-line therapy is freighted with promise but also with dangers, as one generation tampers, however benignly, with the fortunes of another.

## The Religious Setting

The aggressive military image for medicine provides its own standards for criticizing its excesses and stupidities. Every cadet at West Point hears about the outrageous ingenuities of Burnside, Crassus, and Custer. But the more important question still awaits exploration: not the question of moral choices within a model but the moral limits of the model itself. These limits do not show up clearly if we retain too moralistic an understanding of the image's source. Physicians have not imposed the military model on a resistant populace. On the contrary, the model partly emerges in response to the metaphysical pressure people perceive in their lives. The destructiveness of disease, suffering, and death leads victims to enlist the physician as fighter and provokes in patients and families that apprehensive passivity with which they rely on the physician and magic bullets.

Like the parental image of the healer, the contemporary military image presupposes a specific religious reflex before the threat of death. The *summum malum* of violent death has replaced God as the effective center of religious consciousness in the modern world. Perceived as absolute evil, death generates three responses toward itself roughly comparable to the three basic attitudes toward God in the Western religious tradition. First, as we have seen, it produces an inversion of traditional faith in a kind of religious preoccupation with death, a fascination with it, a readiness to draw near it for the sake of the magnification of life that it provides. The therapeutic movement largely associated with Elisabeth Kübler Ross reflects this quest for the authentically human in the experience of dying.

Second, it produces the religious reflex of avoidance, the need to find shelter from threatening and destructive power before which one feels resourceless. This response of avoidance reinforces and deforms the parental image of the healer.

The image of the fighter answers to a third basic reaction to destructive power. As Gerardus van der Leeuw has pointed out, the titan presumptuously rebels against the powerfulness of the sacred by attempting to seize power for himself. Such a person does not, like the philistine, pretend that the sacred does not exist. "On the contrary: power is here frankly recognized and then a hostile attitude is adopted amounting to contempt; and thus man turns away from the power that arouses dread toward himself and toward his own powerfulness."[4] Camus self-consciously rejected the responses of piety and avoidance and defined authentic human existence wholly by a resistance to death. That religious-moral impulse lies behind the medical campaign against death.

But now a complication emerges. Sometimes we experience destructive power wholly as the threat of death; the experience of suffering merely embellishes it. At other times, the ordeal of suffering looms distinct from the fear of death. The *summum malum* now appears in two differing forms, depending on whether suffering or the fear of death grips the consciousness, and generates two distinct ethical responses. Arthur C. McGill has observed that many movements in ethics separate into those that define absolute evil as death and those that define it as suffering.[5] The group that identifies death as the *summum malum*, when consistent, will likely oppose abortion, euthanasia, and war. The group for which suffering looms as the absolute evil will more likely be willing to pull the plug on an individual life to stop irremediable pain or risk death in war rather than face an intolerable slavery.[6] To the degree that either party shapes medical practice, the goal of medicine defines itself negatively and adversarially as being either to prevent suffering or to prevent death.

Each group probably develops its own reflexive sense of a specific preeminent good. When death terrifies as the absolute evil, life seems sacred. When suffering intensifies to intolerable levels, wealth, abundance, or quality of life seems more important than life itself. Thus the moral and political debate polarizes: One group abhors death and holds life sacred; the other abhors suffering and values quality of life over life. Both revere a creaturely good, not the Creator.

## The Christian Setting

Monotheism permits the believer to recognize only God as sacred, creatures as good but not God; they derive from God. Life is a fundamental good, but not absolute; quality of life is to be prized, but not above all else. For this reason, the theist cannot subscribe to the slogan of that most famous of pro-lifers, Albert Schweitzer: "Reverence for Life," which makes life indeterminately divine. (To his credit, Schweitzer had the courage of his convictions. Because he committed himself to life rather than to quality of life, he subordinated his dazzling careers as a musician, composer, philosopher, theologian, and scholar to his vocation as a physician at Lambarene in equatorial Africa.) But neither can the theist accept the opposing absolute: an unconditional reverence for quality of life. That commitment has prompted some of its more narcissistic adherents today to deal ruthlessly with the impoverished and the helpless.

This conventional theist criticism, albeit acceptable, does not go far enough. It does not address the more absorbing problem for the modern psyche and therefore for medical practice. The threat of evil—more than the glitter of creaturely goods—preoccupies the modern consciousness. The current commitments to life and quality of life reflect deeper apprehensions about the absolute evils of death and suffering. Hence, the theistic tradition must assert more relevantly that God transcends not simply the perceived goods of life and quality of life but also the evils of disease, suffering, failure, and death.

In the Christian setting, these evils appear *real*, but not *ultimate*. The events at the very center of Christian consciousness—the passion, death, and resurrection of Jesus—drive the Christian to this metaphysical "assessment" of evil. The Christian reckons in Jesus with the full destructive reality of suffering and death. They cannot be ignored because the passion of Jesus itself narratively insists that suffering and death cannot be avoided, eliminated, or repressed. At the same time, the account of his dying also exposes the ultimate impotence of suffering and death to separate men and women from God. Jesus opens up in the very midst of these events a perduring love. Thus, men and women need not cling fiercely to life or quality of life as the only alternatives to absolute nullity.

In the Christian theist setting, neither life nor wealth of life can command as an absolute good; neither death nor suffering can threaten as an absolute evil, that is, as powerful enough to deprive human beings of the absolutely good. The theistic setting finally relativizes both goods and ills. We can freely enjoy goods, but must not utterly and irrevocably despair at their loss; we should resist evil, but not as though in this resistance alone we find our final resource.

This religious perspective does not always generate unique moral guidelines. Its moral impact is often indirect rather than direct but no less important for that reason. The atmosphere or setting in which men and women act affects mightily the spirit in which they act, their resources, and their resilience. It clears away the despair of those who believe that except for life, we face only death or, except for quality of life, we stare at nothing more than the final humiliation of poverty. The moral life no longer demands a grim visage in the struggle of life against death or "quality of life" against poverty. Political life no longer reduces to a fierce conflict between pro-lifers and quality-of-lifers, each heaping epithets on the other, each charging the other with moral blindness. Both sides shout too shrilly to curb their advocates' excesses: one group clamoring in panic for life at all costs; the other proclaiming, give me quality of life or give me (or them) death. A theological perspective suggests that moral decisions should vary in different cases: sometimes to relieve suffering; at other times to resist death. But in any event, decisions should never reflect that fear and despair from which absolutism derives.

The theistic setting yields two general policy consequences that modify the military model for medical practice. First, the destructive reality of suffering and death provides theological warrant for the struggle against these evils. Fighting these real evils makes Christian sense. However, these evils, although real, are not ultimate. Therefore, they do not justify an absolutely unconditional medical struggle against suffering and death.

The theological warrant for the struggle against suffering and death needs emphasis in order to protect against two versions of Christian piety that would undercut the fight altogether. Some pietists sentimentally misinterpret the suffering and death of Jesus and suffuse them with a romantic religious glow. They confuse Christianity with a *thanatolatry* and a *dolorolatry*, a worship of death and suffering. This view urges on the suffering and the dying the response of acceptance, pure and simple. It elevates suffering to the ennobling and dying to the darkly fulfilling. A pietistic love of suffering and death (*Liebesleid* and *Liebestod*) pervades the soul.

This religious romanticism differs strikingly from the realism of the biblical narrative. Jesus calls his disciples to the way of the cross—but to a life of aggressive, active, self-expending love, not passive, quiescent submission to death. Jesus healed the sick, cleansed the lepers, cast out demons, and raised a young woman from death to life. He used a frankly military image for his contest with demonic power: "But if it is by the finger of God that I cast out demons, then the kingdom of God has come upon you. When a strong man, fully armed, guards his own palace, his goods are in peace;

but when one stronger than he assails him and overcomes him, he takes away his armor in which he trusted, and divides his spoil" (Luke 11:20–22). The speaker of these words is descended from a fighting king; he aggressively heals and, far from wallowing in affliction, prays, "Let this cup pass from me." The early church so emphasized his struggle with afflictive power that its theologians developed what they called the military theory of the atonement. Salvation liberated the sinner from external and destructive power; it did not merely transform inner attitudes. The Gospels provide ample warrant for physician, nurse, and patient to fight disease and death.

The emphasis on the resurrection, however, has led to a second group of Christian pietists who—once again mistakenly—undercut the struggle against suffering and death not by worshiping them but by ignoring them altogether through a triumphalistic understanding of the resurrection. Death and suffering fade before the brilliance of the victory. Deathless life in the risen Lord eliminates wholly the sting of death in the flesh. It also removes the Christian from the daily moral need to spill out life for the brother and the sister. One so emphasizes present participation in eternal life that suffering and death fade away and one begins to demand the psychologically impossible. The pietist expects to face death in a way in which Jesus did not meet his own death—without a tremor. Worse, some Christians expect to walk into a sickroom and "talk up" a victory in a war to those who await an imminent defeat.

Calvin once opposed this professional Christian cheerfulness by observing that the resurrection does not relieve the Christian of natural sorrow. The Christian knows grief in this life. One does not enjoy, on this side of the grave, a pure, confident, and transparent sense of one's limits before God. Death remains in some degree the last enemy, to be resisted and not merely accepted with stoic piety. Salvation is fully consummated only in the future tense. Death, on this side of the grave, still retains its sting. "When the perishable puts on the imperishable . . . , then shall come to pass the saying that is written: 'Death is swallowed up in victory.' O death, where is thy victory? O death, where is thy sting?" (1 Cor. 15:54–55). The careful insertion of the future tense in this passage warns against versions of theistic piety that would denigrate as impious any and all forms of resistance to death.

Christian conviction, on the other hand, prohibits a commitment to an unconditional fight against death. The medical profession should not define itself wholly by the effort to prolong life at any cost. The profession should be free to respond to patients' requests to cease and desist in the medical struggle when the patient has fought the good fight and finished the course and medical resistance can no longer serve his or her health. Thou shalt not kill, indeed, but also needst not strive, officiously, to keep alive—a Christian moralist once observed. Under some circumstances, the physician engaged in primary care may even find ways (as Dr. Eric Cassell has put it) to assist some patients to consent to their own deaths.[7] A physician need not fight pneumonia if the patient has accepted such death in preference to extraordinarily painful, irreversible, and protracted cancer. There is, after all, a time to live and a time to die, and a right to die well. Although the progressive impoverishment of the patient does not in and of itself humiliate (the patient may respond to this ordeal with the dignity of humility rather than humiliation), the event of dying does humiliate if the zeal of others gratuitously prolongs it.[8]

At the same time, however, neither physicians nor the society at large ought to prize quality of life so highly that they solve the problem of suffering by eliminating the sufferer. The advocates of euthanasia often propose this solution to the problem of evil. They doubt patients' capacity to cope once terminal pain and suffering have appeared. They assume that life has peaked somewhere on a hill behind them and that all else ahead slopes downward toward oblivion. They doubt that end-time itself can be suffused with the human.

### Justifiable War and Hospital Policies

These general guidelines, if accepted, affect the discussion of distinctions important to hospital and professional policies, the distinctions between (1) maximal care and optimal care; and (2) allowing to die, assisted suicide, and mercy killing.

*1. Maximal Care and Optimal Care.* A policy that urges an all-out war against death presupposes that maximal treatment offers optimal care. We must doubt, however, that maximal medical assault by invasive diagnostic procedures, by aggressive and complicated drug management, by enthusiastic cutting and burning optimally serves the patient. Often such treatment merely distracts the patient and family from using precious time for what really matters. At worst, the therapeutically battered patient resembles the Vietnamese village that American bombs flattened in the course of "liberating" it. Fortunately, therefore, some teaching hospitals—precisely those institutions whose resources would most tempt them to wage an all-out battle—have pulled back from total war against death.

The Massachusetts General Hospital (MGH) has adopted procedures recommended by its Critical Care Committee that would limit medical war by classifying critically ill patients into four groups:

Class A:  *Maximal therapeutic effort with reservation.*

Class B:  *Maximal therapeutic effort without reservation but with daily evaluation.*

Class C:  *Selective limitation of therapeutic measures.* A Class C patient is not an appropriate candidate for admission to an intensive care unit.

Class D:  *All therapy can be discontinued* . . . although maximum comfort to the patient may be continued or instituted.[9]

The Massachusetts General Hospital Report, by implication at least, dissolves two distinctions that previously established for some physicians and moralists clear-cut limits on therapeutic efforts: the distinctions between starting and stopping machines and between ordinary and heroic measures. In my judgment, the report correctly abandons both distinctions for the more apt criterion of the patient's welfare.

*a.* Physicians commonly feel that they exercise discretion in a case only until they start the machines. Once machines are running, they lose the option of letting the patient die. This position offers more security legally and psychologically. Once the physician restores vital signs, it seems like killing to pull the plug. The distinction has the practical disadvantage of encouraging physicians not to start the machines for fear of producing grotesque results over which they no longer have control. Freedom to turn off the machines would allow them to put more patients on the machines in the first place in order to make a more informed choice. Put another way, the distinction misleads to the degree that it converts a machine from an instrument into a fatality. It falsely assumes that a running machine has escaped the reach of human decision making. It is no longer anyone's responsibility.

This quiescent attitude toward the equipment repeats the more general submissiveness that the patient (even if competent) and his or her family feel toward the hospital staff. The patient feels fully free to make decisions only before going into the facility. Once within, the patient feels gauche when questioning routines and procedures. Like the visitor at the whorehouse, the patient tends to feel that, once past the front door, one has to go along with what goes on there. It is hard to back out.

The MGH Report subordinates the operation of machines to the patient's welfare; it allows for the reclassification of patients and provides for daily evaluation of patients in Class B. The report also establishes procedures for such acts as turning off mechanical ventilators at that point in therapy when the machine may offer maximal treatment but not optimal care.

*b.* Similarly, the MGH Report implies rejection of the medical distinction between ordinary and heroic measures, on the basis of which physicians (and patients and their families) can decide to withhold life-prolonging therapy only if it can be characterized as heroic. This distinction between the ordinary and the heroic appeals morally insofar as it allows some patients to die, but it rests too heavily on the "heroic" status of the means. If it can be said conscientiously in a given case that the withdrawal of heroic measures best serves the patient's well-being, then in some circumstances the withdrawal of a treatment as ordinary today as penicillin may serve as well.

The MGH Report, in effect, relaxes the distinction between ordinary and heroic when it provides for Classification D, under which all therapy (but not all efforts to provide comfort) can be discontinued. The crucial distinction should not fall between ordinary and heroic measures, but between two sorts of patients with two differing conditions and sets of needs: those for whom efforts toward cure may succeed, and those for whom efforts at remedy will fail but for whom care remains imperative. As Paul Ramsey has said: "The right medical practice will provide those who may get well with the assistance they need, and it will provide those who are dying with the care and assistance they need in their final passage. To fail to distinguish between these two sorts of medical practice would be to fail to act in accordance with the facts."[10]

A given procedure, whether ordinary or heroic, should be evaluated as to whether it offers optimal care or merely maximal treatment. Full-throttle efforts to cure or to keep alive may in fact neglect the patient, gagging that person with the irrelevant, while denying what he or she truly needs. It may overlook the patient's real condition and wants: "Just as it would be negligence to the sick to treat them as if they were about to die, so it is another sort of 'negligence' to treat the dying as if they are going to get well or might get well."[11] The MGH Report, with its provision for daily evaluations, attempts to eliminate the negligence of misplaced treatment.

The MGH guidelines emphasize the needs and welfare of the patient but pay almost no attention, at least directly, to the question of the patient's right to make decisions. The guidelines assume that the staff will make most decisions *on behalf of patients*. Although the patient and his or her family, along with many other parties, can initiate questions about treatment classification, the final decision rests with the attending physician. Others do not have an acknowledged or regularized place in making those decisions—not, at least, in the published version of the procedures.[12]

The MGH Report does not evince that systematic and scrupulous respect for the competent patient and family that the Beth Israel Hospital of Boston demonstrates in its "Orders Not to Resuscitate."[13] While declaring the hospital's general policy to "act affirmatively to preserve the life of all patients," the Beth Israel document acknowledges those situations in which heroic measures "might be both medically unsound and so contrary to the patient's wishes or expectations as not to be justified." The document then establishes procedures by which the competent patient (or family, in the case of an incompetent patient) can collaborate in a standing order not to resuscitate—specifically, in those cases that satisfy the conditions of irreversibility, irreparability, and imminence of death.

The Beth Israel document formally provides for patient consent to treatment. Still, to what degree do patients want to exercise this right when it comes down to their own dying? Much well-intentioned medical practice operates on the conviction that the liberty to deal with one's own dying is an unwanted liberty. The physician, for example, who brought the series of articles in *The New England Journal of Medicine* to my attention expressed doubts about the readiness of patients to participate in decisions about their own death. He commented candidly that he "liked" the Report of Massachusetts General Hospital, but found the "other" policy statement that sought patient concurrence in such matters ghoulish. His judgment reflects a widely shared skepticism about the likelihood that patients will find it a favor to be confronted with the question of their courage in the face of death. Informed consent remains pro forma if the patient will not face his or her own dying. The patient signs the papers quickly because he or she will not entertain the prospect of a medical failure and a personal disaster.

Thus the issue of informed consent poses more deeply the question of the human possibility for dignity, humility, and courage in facing death; knowledgeable consent to procedures that may go awry rests on a willingness at some level to face one's own dying. The insistence on the right to die springs from some sense of the duty to die well. Lacking either that sense of duty or the confidence that one could possibly discharge it well, the patient reflexively throws the initiative back to the physician and staff to press on with the fight against death and perhaps even to maintain the illusion, however meager the evidence, that the fight goes well.

2. *Allowing to Die, Assisted Suicide, and Mercy Killing.* Some moralists, such as Joseph Fletcher, believe that those who would distinguish among allowing to die, assisted suicide, and mercy killing quibble hypocritically over technique.[14] Because the patient dies— whether by acts of omission or commission—what matters the route? By either procedure, the patient ends up dead. Proponents of assisted suicide and euthanasia, as indicated earlier, give priority to the fight against suffering over the fight against death. They confer death in order to spare suffering. They believe that respect for the patient's autonomy should govern the care of the dying. If we legally prohibit

euthanasia, we fail to respect the liberty of those who want the doctor's assistance in ending their dying. It's a free country, and freedom ought to extend to the choice of one's final exit. The patient who consents to being killed or asks assistance in suicide presumably harms no other person. Thus a legal prohibition against assisted suicide or euthanasia seems unjustified and arbitrary. Second, proponents appeal to the compassion of the caregiver with the term "mercy killing." Lacking the option of euthanasia, we do not act as compassionately as we might; we impose gratuitous suffering on the terminally ill.

The movement advocating assisted suicide gathered force toward the end of the twentieth century. In 1994, the state of Oregon adopted a measure that allows terminally ill patients to obtain a prescription for lethal drugs to end their lives. Patients initiating the request must be capable, and a consenting physician must have determined that the patient suffers from a terminal disease. Various other safeguards aim at securing the fully informed and uncoerced decision and protect doctors from adverse consequences should they choose not to prescribe lethal drugs. As of 2000, the Orgeon measure had not yet spread to other states; however, Americans, including church people, seem closely divided on the issue.

Other moralists, opposed to euthanasia, would preserve the distinction between allowing to die and mercy killing and favor the former. This position can be defended in two ways, either by exploring the obligations of the community to the dying or by examining the rights and duties of the dying.

Most proponents of allowing to die begin with the obligations of the community, particularly those of medical professionals to give appropriate care. This imperative sets a limit on the efforts to fight death by simply prolonging the process of dying. It justifies allowing to die. There comes a time when physicians, family, and friends must cease their efforts to fight death, not to abandon the patient, but to provide care and only care. More aggressive treatment under some conditions misses the mark and ultimately neglects the patient. This line of reasoning, however, would not extend the mandate of care to mercy killing. To care in the form of killing rejects the obligation to care by eliminating the patient. While the irreversibly dying live, they claim from us care and not something else—neither officious efforts to prolong their lives nor shortcuts to end them. Mercy killing, in its own inverted way, abandons patients.

In appealing to respect for autonomy and compassion as the basis for their position, euthanasianists face serious practical difficulties. Viewed as an expansion of the patient's right to determine his or her own destiny, the practice of voluntary euthanasia may reflect an extremely naive view of the uncoerced nature of the decision. The decision and plea to be killed is hardly an unforced decision if the terms and conditions under which we deliver care for the dying are already woefully mistargeted, inadequate, or downright neglectful. When elderly patients have stumbled around in apartments, alone and frightened for decades, when they have spent years warehoused in geriatrics barracks, when they have not been visited by relatives for months, or when relatives dump them off in emergency rooms to be rid of them for a holiday, then the decision to be killed for mercy hardly reflects an uncoerced decision. Their alternative may be so wretched, repellent, and distasteful as to push some patients toward this death to resolve their plight.

It is a huge irony and, in some cases, hypocrisy, to urge a compassionate killing, when we have starved aged and dying people of compassion for many of their declining years. To put it bluntly, a country has not earned the moral option to kill for mercy in good conscience if it has not already sustained and supported life with compassion and mercy. Active euthanasia could become a final solution for handling the problem of the aged poor. (It warrants recalling that over 40 million citizens of the United States lack health care insurance. It is the only industrialized country other than South Africa that so denies a major portion of its citizens acute care. Active euthanasia might provide too many people an offer they might feel, given the alternative, that they could not refuse.)

Further, the test of compassion lies, not in investing yet more money in acute care facilities, but rather in shifting substantial amounts to preventive medicine, rehabilitative medicine, long-term and terminal care, and strategic home services, which would provide patients with a humane alternative to a quick death. Otherwise our society cumulatively kills, not for compassion, but for convenience and to reduce the demands on our compassion. By denying adequate provision for chronic care and home assistance, our society nudges not only the solitary, neglected patient toward the exit but also the patient who watches his old, tired, and overburdened mate painfully attempt to give him care without any humane respite. This statement about compassion does not charge a doctor or family member in a given case with less than the purest motives. The test of compassion is not simply the individual case but the cumulative impact of a social policy.

Our social covenant obligates us to provide care always. Most of the time, care takes the form of treatment. At some point, treatment no longer serves the patient's well being. But even when we cease to treat, our social covenant requires that we continue to care. Unceasing care is the moral principle behind allowing to die.

Thus laws prohibiting euthanasia should be accompanied by full and proper use of allowing to die. The patient's welfare and his or her rights to refuse treatment should govern not only starting the machines but also stopping them, not only withholding treatment but also withdrawing it, not only the use of extraordinary means but also the employment of ordinary means. Otherwise allowing to die can lead to inappropriate treatment and patient abuse.

Expanding the doctor's discretionary power to allow the patient to die does not of itself address the pain and suffering of the still dying patient. Thus prohibitions against euthanasia and assisted suicide impose an even more intense responsibility to make sure that no patients, especially those who are being allowed to die, are abandoned to pain. As efforts to treat cease, efforts to care for, make comfortable, and console must intensify. Dr. Joanne Lynn, a distinguished hospice physician, has specified some of the details of humane care, which our obsession with TV–spectacular medicine has tempted us to neglect: using drugs effectively to control pain; adroitly managing various symptoms, gastrointestinal, respiratory, and agonal; treating skin problems, fever, and weakness; encouraging mental alertness.[15] These prosaic tasks, which high-tech medicine has tended to dismiss as hand-holding, are part of the modest covenantal efficaciousness of care.

Medical research and education have not focused sufficiently on the pressing needs of the dying. As Dr. Lynn elsewhere complained, "Often 'it is easier to get a heart transplant or cataract surgery than supper or a back rub,' let alone effective pain relief."[16] Dr. Kevorkian could engage in overtreating his patients with assisted suicide, because he attracted those who had been undertreated for depression. We generally under-evaluate, and thus mistreat, the dying. Some 81 percent of doctors conceded in a survey reported in a *New York Times* editorial that "the most common form of narcotic abuse in the care of the dying is the undertreatment of pain."[17] Only one in ten physicians, in a 1989 study conducted by Dr. Jamie H. Von Roenn of Northwestern University, "said they received good training in managing pain."[18] Only one-fifth of 1 percent of the billion dollar budget of the National Cancer Institute goes to research on reducing pain. Instead of covenantally caring appropriately for dying people, the euthanasia movement tempts us to swing smoothly from aggressive treatment aimed at keeping patients alive to equally aggressive treatment at killing them.

The second, less conventional, defense of the distinction between allowing to die and killing for mercy focuses on the patient's rather than the professional's obligations. Modern teachers in the field of medical ethics are almost mute on the subject of the patient's virtues. Medical ethics concentrates exclusively on the ethics of the caregiver, but not those of the care receiver. It emphasizes the patients' rights but not the patients' duties. We may subtly dehumanize patients when we do not take seriously the question of their virtues and vices, the nobility or meanness of their responses to ordeal. We act and reflect as though the patient does not have a moral life.

We cannot, of course, discuss the question of the patient's duty to die well without reckoning with the features of a good death. To its credit, the euthanasia movement has reintroduced the patient into the discussion of medical ethics because the movement poses, at least in principle, the question of what constitutes a good death. It gives, however, a peculiarly modern answer to that question, partly in response to the modern religious atmosphere and partly in reaction to the excesses of the unconditional fight against death.

Most modern people equate a good death with a sudden death. They want to go quickly in an accident; they prefer a heart attack to cancer. As the tavern sign puts the modern credo:

> Here's to a long life
> And a merry one
> A quick death and an easy one
> A pretty girl and a true one
> A cold beer and another one.

To the best of my knowledge, Søren Kierkegaard in the nineteenth century first drew attention to the modern preference for a sudden death.[19] He correlated the preference with a decline in religious seriousness. The preference intensified in the twentieth century with the development of a medical technology that cruelly prolongs the dying process. Further and ironically, the modern world simultaneously produced a desire for a sudden death and the incredibly expensive diagnostic tools and genetic screening devices that provide an early warning system about diseases, many irremediable. The physician sits, sometimes uncomfortably, on top of this unwanted information. The preference for a quick death has spread so widely today that almost any other choice seems incomprehensible. If, of course, no other choice is truly intelligible, then one might be more inclined to collapse the distinction between active and passive euthanasia and go the quickest route possible.

Yet historically, another preference is possible. We know, for example, that people in the Middle Ages preferred some advance warning about their death. Conversely, they listed a sudden death among the many evils from which devout folk should pray for deliverance. Clearly, people want a warning if they feel that they can, in some way, prepare for an event. Hosts deem it unfortunate when a guest catches them partly dressed and without something in the pantry. One would prefer a little time to prepare for the occasion. The traditional prayers of the church shrewdly acknowledged a link between warning and preparation. The Rogation Day service listed evils from which the believer prayed for deliverance; it included the evil of a *sudden and unprovided-for* death. Conversely, a good death included warning and very specific preparations,[20] a forewarning that invited one to prepare for and take over one's own dying.

However, the euthanasia movement encourages engineering death rather than facing dying. Euthanasia would bypass dying to get one dead as quickly as possible. It proposes to relieve suffering by knocking out the interval between the two states of life and death. The moral impulse behind the movement understandably responds to the quandaries of an age that makes of dying such an inhumanly endless business. However, the movement opposes the horrors of a purely technical death by using technique to eliminate the victim.

In a different moral and religious setting, warning can provoke some measure of good; with time for preparation, some reconciliation can take place; and advanced grieving by those about to suffer loss may ease some pain. Studies have noted that those bereaved who lose someone accidentally or suddenly face more difficulties in recovering from the loss than those who have suffered through a period of illness before the death. Those who have lost a close relative by accident will, more likely, experience what Geoffrey Gorer has called limitless grief.[21] The community, moreover, needs its aged and dependent, its sick and dying, and the virtues that they sometimes evince—the virtues of humility, courage, and patience—just as much as the community needs the virtues of justice and love manifest in the agents of its care. Thus, on the whole, I am in favor of social policy that takes seriously the notion of allowing to die, rather than killing for mercy, that is, that recognizes that moment in illness when it makes no sense, other than technical, to bend every effort to prolong life and when we can decorously allow patients to do their own dying. This policy seems most consonant with the obligations of the community to care and the necessity of the patient to finish his or her course.

I can, to be sure, imagine rare circumstances in which I hope I would have the courage to kill for mercy—when the patient is irreversibly beyond human care, terminal, and in extreme and unabatable pain. A neurosurgeon once showed a seminar group the picture of a Vietnam casualty who had lost all four limbs in a land-mine explosion. The catastrophe had reduced him to a trunk with his face transfixed in horror. On the battlefield, I hope I would have the courage to cross the boundary and kill the sufferer with mercy. But hard cases do not always make good laws or wise social policies. Regularized mercy killings would too quickly and cheaply relieve the community of its obligation to provide good care. Who ever said the moral life is easy?

By admitting the possibility of an exception to a general prohibition against euthanasia, I will probably please relativists and trouble absolutists. At first glance, relativists and absolutists seem radically opposed to each other. Relativists deny and absolutists uphold the validity of moral principles. But at a deeper level, they resemble each another. Both believe that the existence of an exception or a counterinstance undercuts the validity of a principle. Relativists seize on the exception as reason for dissolving the principle. Absolutists deny the exception or counterinstances in order to sustain the principle. Both fail to recognize the wisdom of Aristotle's observation that moral principles are true for the most part. They have general, not universal, validity. The existence of some exceptions to a principle does not of itself destroy its validity or the laws based on it. The recognition of some territorial limits to a principle, as it yields to a more urgent consideration in a particular case, should not of itself blot out the territory the principle covers. The rare exception to the general prohibition against euthanasia should not of itself undercut the moral considerations that underlie the prohibition.

We should not always expect the law to provide us with full protection and coverage for what, in rare circumstances, we may morally need to do. Sometimes, the moral life calls us out into a no-man's land where we cannot expect total security and protection under the law. Were I ever to find myself in the situation in which I felt that I must euthanize someone, I would think it best not to seek advance legal protection but to recognize that what I was taking on myself was to throw myself on the mercy of the court. As a practical matter, that would tend to minimize the number of instances of active euthanasia. All things considered, it is best that the practice be rare.

## Chapter Three

# Technician

The modern medical establishment has largely justified itself as a war department. It fights against disease and against suffering, impairment, and death, which follow in its wake. But medical professionals, like their counterparts in a professional army, hardly keep the banner of the large cause foremost before them as they perform their daily tasks. They attend to the immediate demands for excellence in technical performance. Idealistic volunteers may join the army for noble reasons, but professionals find themselves occupied enough with keeping their guns well oiled and the troops in fighting trim. Excellent technical performance becomes the effective center of the professional ethic.

Contemporary philosophers and theologians writing on medical ethics have said little that is positive about a professional ethic that prizes, above all else, excellence in the practice of the art. Utilitarianism deals with action as purely instrumental to preferred outcomes. It does not reckon with the intrinsic significance of the action itself.[1] As such, it misses altogether the interior experience of the professional who finds meaning in performance per se. A Kantian ethic of duty also subordinates technique. It distinguishes between merely hypothetical imperatives (directed to actions "practically necessary as a means to the attainment of something else")[2] and a categorical imperative (directed to action "objectively necessary in itself apart from its relation to a further end").[3] In either case, philosophers reduce technical skill to a secondary and subordinate place. They do not reckon with that professional ideal for which the result of a deed fades in significance before the beauty of the deed itself. Not until professional ethics reckons with the ideal of technical performance and its moral power will medical ethics seem more than marginal to professional education and practice.

Novelists have more to offer than do philosophers and theologians on the ethic of technical performance. I recommend Rudyard Kipling and Ernest Hemingway as patron saints for the prevailing ethic among medical practitioners today. Each celebrates an important aspect of those ideals that determine current medical education and clinical training and govern subsequent practice.

Of the two authors, Kipling provides the more convenient transition from the preoccupations of the last chapter to the concerns of this one. The more old fashioned of the two writers, Kipling had not yet wearied of war or of the goods that flow from its successful pursuit. He highly prized both an imperial cause served and the technology through which one serves it. He celebrated war and empire but also gloried in the professional—the engineer, the soldier, the financier —whose technical skill made possible its victories, whether in subduing other peoples or in conquering space. His poem "McAndrew's Hymn" nicely brings together the two themes of globe-encircling empire and technical skill. The speaker in that poem, a Scottish engineer, derives a double pleasure—both in his service to the ship's passengers, which he performs by doing his duty, and in the well-working of the engines over which he watches:

> Obsairve. Per annum we'll have here
> two thousand souls aboard—
> Think not I dare to justify myself before the Lord,
> But—average fifteen hunder souls
> safe-borne fra' port to port—
> I am o' service to my kind. Ye wadna
> blame the thought?[4]

With just a touch of self-pity, he prides himself in the anonymity of that service. The passengers, as they leave, have

> words for every one but me—
> shake hands wi' half the crew,
> Except the dour Scots engineer,
> the man they never knew.[5]

He finds satisfaction in service, but technology and technical performance supply his ultimate justification. The engineer lives in and through the engines he tends:

> Lord, send a man like Robbie Burns to
> sing the Song o' Steam!
> To match wi' Scotia's noblest speech
> yon orchestra sublime
> Whaurto—uplifted like the Just—
> the tail-rods mark the time.
> The crank-throws give the double-bass,
> the feed-pump sobs an' heaves,
> An' now the main eccentrics start their
> quarrel on the sheaves:

Her time, her own appointed time, the
   rocking link-head bides,
Till—hear that note?—the rod's return
   whings glimmerin' through the guides.
They're all awa'! True beat, full power,
   the clangin' chorus goes
Clear to the tunnel where they sit,
   my purrin' dynamos.
Interdependence absolute, foreseen, ordained,
   decreed, To work, Ye'll note, at ony
     tilt an' every rate o' speed.[6]

    In a sense, the cause cannot fade because the cause itself fuses with the technical performance that so exuberantly serves it. The purring of the dynamos makes possible British hegemony over other cultures and nations; and technology itself partly supplies the substance to that civilization. Thus means overreach ends because the end itself has become the sweet-sounding virtuosity of the technological means (and of those professionals who forge them, use them, and enjoy them—capitalists, soldiers, and engineers). Behind Kipling's rhapsodic celebration of the triumph of modern technological civilization (in its British form) lies the Baconian vision, some four centuries old, that ushered in the modern era. Francis Bacon linked together Knowledge, Power, and Philanthropy, a kind of holy trinity, from which latter-day professionals derive their authority and prestige. Kipling comes at the end of a long line of Boy Scouts, extending from Francis Bacon of the early seventeenth century to the First World War, men who had faith in the links between knowledge, transformative power, and service to humankind. The knowledge they prized did more than deepen wisdom after the fashion of the tragedians; it enlarged human capacities; it produced technology; it lent itself to industrial application. This wondrous enlargement of human power should, could, and would serve humankind. This humanitarian faith in knowledge, power, and philanthropy furnished the modern world with the professional as hero: the engineer, the doctor, the soldier, and the market expert. Knowledge itself offered a treasure house that, through technique, would transform the world for the better. In this respect, the modern professional differs from the ancient sage who offered wisdom but not power and from the wizard-magician who wielded the power of esoteric knowledge but sometimes only to exhibit his own virtuosity.

Both the technological triumphalism that Kipling celebrated and the civilization that largely powered it faced major bumps on the road in the twentieth century. The western nations grew in technological power only to turn their industrial might against one another in World War I and then again in World War II. In the interval between the wars, the engines of progress wheezed and shuddered to a halt in the great depression of the 1930s. The postwar period through the 1990s saw a resurgence of industry and technology; but the mushroom cloud of nuclear war hung over the decades; and, from the 1960s forward, critics and citizens worried about the huge costs and destructive side effects that the human effort to master nature would impose both on nature and on those who sought to master it. The woes that technological triumphalism generated on a global scale repeated some of the griefs aggressive medicine imposed on patients in its campaign against disease and death.

We have already placed this Promethean project to push against the limits of human life in the setting of the religious tradition of the West. The tradition both authorizes the medical resistance to disease and death and also places limits on the battle. This chapter focuses on a different inspiration for setting limits to the battle. This inspiration grows out of disillusionment with unconditional warfare. It no longer justifies either technology or technical performance by the ends it accomplishes but by the intrinsic value of the performance itself. Ernest Hemingway offers the best insight into an ethics of technical performance that disconnects from the external ends that such performance might serve. He wrote about the world that follows hard on the collapse of Kipling's imperial vision.

Hemingway wrote about the Great War and the Spanish Civil War and the expatriate generation between, and he eloquently recorded the breakup of a civilization that relied on the links between knowledge, transformative power, and philanthropy. In their place, he promulgated a code that centered on performance alone. Like Kipling, Hemingway wrote about soldiers. But his heroes in *A Farewell to Arms* and *For Whom the Bell Tolls* assiduously distance themselves from the causes that put them in the battle. Frederic Henry does not fight in the Great War under Woodrow Wilson's banner of making the world "Safe for Democracy"; and Robert Jordan concedes that he has long since forgotten why he is fighting in the Spanish Civil War.

Some critics thought Hemingway's work expressed moral nihilism. He distrusted all causes spelled with capital letters. As a writer in the 1920s, he let the air out of Wilsonian idealism. An expatriate in Paris, disillusioned with war, cut off from his homeland, suspicious of the ideals that ordinarily organize men and women into enterprises of great moment, he sought in skill some hope of virtue.

Hemingway espoused with moral passion a code that replaced the old allegiances to Country, Justice, Democracy, and the like. The exigencies of battle cut off the hero from the resounding claims of cause. He no longer remembers why he fights, but he lives by a code that requires him to fight well. This code centers less on the ends of action than on its form. The Hemingway hero eats well, drinks well, loves well, hunts well, fishes well, writes well, fights well, and dies well.

In his eloquent defense of a code that centers on technical performance, Hemingway voices the practical commitments of the modern professional. Modern young men and women often enter their profession as Wilsonian idealists or claim as much on their application forms. But as they immerse themselves in the practical demands of their education and apprenticeship, the ideals usually fade; only respect for a job well done remains. Excellence in technical performance marks the professional. Leave it to the amateurs, the civilians, and the politicians to keep alive the old, divisive battle lines that causes draw. A general can admire the tactical skill of an enemy irrespective of the justice of his cause. Lawyers on opposite sides of a courtroom case go off to lunch together after a trial, each respectful of the other's performance. Physicians quickly learn to abstract their interest in a medical case from the fateful issues that the patient and family face. A case intrigues to the degree that it challenges technical skill. Thus the image of the physician as fighter in a just cause recedes before the image of the technician with a justifying skill and with independent appreciation for skill tested under the fire of battle.

The ideal of excellence on technical performance does not surface for the first time in modern medical practice. It traces back the full length of the Western tradition to a Hippocratic root. Two loves energized the physician in classical Greece, according to Pedro Lain Entralgo, the Spanish historian of medicine: *philanthropia* and *philotechnia*, love of humankind and love of the art.[7]

The written codes of the profession emphasize the love of humankind. This love determines a series of duties, negative and positive, in the earliest of written codes. Out of concern for the well-being of the patient, the physician—so the Hippocratic Oath specifies—must not perform surgery, assist patients in attempts at suicide or abortion, break a confidence, or commit acts of injustice or mischief toward the patient and the latter's household, including sexual misconduct. In short, the physician, out of love for humankind, must above all else "do no harm." More positively, however, the physician must always work for the benefit of the sick. This positive injunction develops into the justification of the art of healing *(techni iatriki)*—chiefly dietetics, gymnastics, and drugs.

Thus philanthropy justifies *philotechnia*. From his teacher, the physician-to-be learned something about the construction of a healthy life, the elimination and control of suffering, and the crucial distinction between diseases curable and incurable. In general terms, the art of healing attempted "to do away with the sufferings of the sick, to lessen the violence of their diseases, and to refuse to treat those who are overmastered by their diseases, realizing that in such cases medicine is powerless" *(Hippocratic Corpus, 50.6. 4–6)*. In this latter respect, the Greek tradition differs from the technological triumphalism of the modern (Kipling's) world. The love of technical skill included not only an appreciation of the good that the application of that skill might achieve but also a natural piety that recognized the limits of the art. Only *hybris* (and foolishness) would attempt to force a cure on the incurable. Skillful professionals know their limits and the limits that nature places on them.

The ideal of philanthropy tends to take precedence over the ideal of *philotechnia* in the written codes of the modern medical guild in the United States. The first Code of Medical Ethics, adopted by the American Medical Association (AMA) in 1847, and the more recent formulations of 1957 and forward, portray the physician as philanthropist. The physician makes personal sacrifices out of love for humankind. The 1847 AMA Code refers to the members of the medical profession as those "upon whom is enjoined the performance of so many arduous duties toward the community, and who are required to make so many sacrifices of comfort, ease, and health, for the welfare of those who avail themselves of their services."[8] The words sound a little pretentious today in the light of the tens of thousands of physicians who have enjoyed great comfort and financial ease as a result of their medical practice. Still the ideal of philanthropic service receives its ritual due as the earnest applicants for medical school routinely mention the desire to serve as the motive that has impelled them to seek admission.

But the written codes of a profession determine practice far less than those unwritten codes passed from one generation of practitioners to another in the laboratory or the clinic. Here, competence takes precedence. Skill as a bench scientist in the laboratory or as a practitioner in a clinic takes precedence over the orotund moral ideals that guild publicists invoke in recommending the profession to society.

The criteria for admission to medical school, the grading system that prevails there, the system for the placement of graduates in residencies, and eventual job references—all these hurdles and pressure points combine to emphasize the preeminent place of technical performance in the formation and career of the professional. In both the laboratory and the clinic, moreover, those features of technical performance that lend themselves most to measurement—grades, test scores, number of publications, and so on—tend to determine destiny.

These developments—well enough known, much criticized, and relatively impervious to criticism—favor the technical and the quantitative. Little has been done to explore the moral warrants for the commitment to the ideal of technical performance other than relatively utilitarian appeals to external outcomes. It appears, however, that the ideal commands allegiance even in the face of failure, in which case one needs to explore those goods that are internal to technical practice in order to understand the professional commitment to them. That exploration takes us farther into Hemingway, who saw the link between technical performance, the internal satisfaction it offers, and the protection it affords against tragedy. The event of a bullfight, about which he repeatedly wrote, offers the best access to these themes.

The ritual killing of a bull in Hemingway's short stories and novels symbolizes a world without commitments and ties.

> The bull charged and Villalta charged and just for a moment they became one. Villalta became one with the bull and then it was over.[9]

The young Hemingway, working as a reporter, described the bullfight not as a sport but as a tragedy in three acts.[10] It includes the passing with the cape to distract the bull from the escaping picador, the striking of the bull with three-foot lances to the right and left of the shoulder blades, and the killing of the bull with a thrust beyond the neck and between the shoulder blades. In any event, the bull does not usually escape with its life. The bullfight presents in cameo form the world that the war novels and the expatriate stories have already revealed. War rules out long-term ties. Hemingway writes about lovers, but rarely about enduring marriage or the family. Catherine in *A Farewell to Arms* and Robert Jordan in *For Whom the Bell Tolls* inevitably must die. Just for a moment, lovers become one, and then it is over.

The bullfighter, the wartime lover, the expatriate—all alike—live by a code that eschews involvement; for each there comes a time when the thing is over; death terminates. But this does not mean that men and women cannot live beautifully, stylishly, fittingly in the midst of impermanence and death. The bullfighter works "gracefully, effortlessly, and with dignity."[11] The emphasis falls on the aesthetic. The bullfighter, par excellence, symbolizes concern for the form of action rather than its content or end. Causes fade, persons die, the bottle empties, partners fall away, the moment ends; it cannot shape the future. Stylish performance alone counts. Particular virtues push in the direction of the aesthetic. Courage is grace under pressure. In learning to drink, love, hunt, and die well, the "well" has an aesthetic ring to it. The moral ritualizes into deeds beautifully performed.

Yet this aesthetic ideal has its moral implications. Beautiful performance requires discipline. There is a right and a wrong way to do things. The wrong way usually results from a faulty technique or from an excessive preoccupation with one's ego. The bad bull-fighter either lacks technique or lets his ego—through fear or vanity—obstruct his performance. Either he refuses, out of fear, to expose himself to the limits of danger, or, grandstanding for the audience, he exceeds those limits. Technical proficiency and a style wholly purified of disruptive preoccupation with oneself supply the moral conditions of beauty. The later novel *The Old Man and the Sea* deepens this code to a tragic limit. After a long stretch in which he has caught no fish, the old fisherman goes after a big marlin alone and at length catches the fish and lashes it to the boatside to bring it home, but he loses it to sharks on the shoreward haul because he "went out too far," he exceeded his limit. With that phrase, Hemingway recovers for *philotechnia* that element of piety toward nature that the modern triumphalists have obscured but that the Greeks always understood: a sense of one's limits before daunting challenge.

In addition to its aesthetic content and its moral prerequisites, the Hemingway code also performs a psychological function. The patterning of behavior serves to protect the vulnerable ego. The Hemingway hero, especially as imitated in the movies and other media, gives the impression of being a tough guy without feelings or a stoic who has reached a state of apathy beyond all feeling. That caricature misses the point. His heroes feel keenly for what they hunt, fish, and make love to. The old man speaks of the big fish as his brother. Imminent death heightens feeling. Robert Jordan in *For Whom the Bell Tolls* knows that he will die as he waits for the fascists to come up the road, but he sits positioned, his gun in hand and his leg broken, his senses fully open to the earth he is about to leave. The code hardly serves a deadened sensibility.

Rather, its rituals perform the important psychological function of buffering the ego from losses too difficult to bear without shield.

Furthermore, the code has a social, regulatory function. Those who live by the code distinguish themselves —sometimes cruelly—from those who aspire to but cannot. The Hemingway novel, especially *The Sun Also Rises*, distinguishes ruthlessly between insiders and outsiders, those who do and those who do not have the goods. In this respect, Hemingway only reflects what we already know about the social function of "code words," gestures, and behavior among friends, workers in the same company, or members of an elite social set. They develop special ways of communicating with one another, make privileged demands on one another, and separate themselves thereby from the common lot. They need no written rules. Unwritten patterns of behavior suffice to enforce standards among members and to exclude outsiders.

Finally, the Hemingway code cuts across the ordinary distinction between work and play, vocation and avocation, performances of the professional and those of the amateur. No one displays better the ethic of *philotechnia* than the amateur English fisherman in *The Sun Also Rises*. Hemingway's sports supply more than recreation. He seems to seek those sports that expose the human condition. The hard shadow of death lies across the activities of hunting, fishing, and bullfighting. Not even Hemingway's references to baseball altogether escape the heightening of mortality; his old fisherman constantly invokes the symbol of aging glory. Joe DiMaggio—the hero with hits in fifty-six straight games—has a bone spur, an Achilles heel.

In several ways, the Hemingway code expresses at their best the prevailing ideals of most professions today but particularly that profession that traffics in death. The oncologist, the hematologist, the surgeon, the cardiologist, and the gerontologist constantly deal with death, but so also do those generalists and internists whose patients largely include the aged and the infirm. The daily round of professional experience for the physician and the nurse reinforces a sense that we live in a world that allows no long-term expectations, no enduring ties.

Under these circumstances, a code that centers on technical performance serves an invaluable psychological function. It does not encourage personal involvement with the patient; and it helps free the physician from the destructive consequences of involvement. The professional ideal of compassion sounds plausible enough in its somewhat soft focus as a diffuse sympathy. But in its literal meaning as a "suffering with," compassion also threatens the professional relationship. The physician cannot pretend to act as the second Person of the Trinity who descends vicariously with every patient into his or her particular form of suffering, pain, crucifixion, and hell. It seems prudent enough to offer whatever help one can through finely honed technical services and let the services at the same time provide the physician and the nurse with a kind of leaden shield against a field of radioactive emotions. The professional needs emotional freedom to withdraw the self when these services no longer work, when, as Hemingway would say, "it is over."

The codal ideal of technical excellence also makes its moral demands on the physician. It requires that the professional subordinate the ego, its wants and aversions, to the technical question of how to do a thing and do it well. A good deal of the moral conditioning of medical school directs itself to detaching the young physician-to-be from the vagaries of ordinary human ties. The early placement of the course in gross anatomy (usually in the first year of medical school) presents the young professional with a cadaver before he or she sees a living patient. It suggests that one's science must not diverge from its appointed tasks into the complexities of relationships to the living. ("Let the social worker take care of that" echoes along the hospital corridors.) The very structure of daily rounds and floor service reinforces for residents the importance of breaking ties with patients. Residents get acquainted with particular patients whose histories they have taken and whom they monitor daily. But the ritual of morning rounds and the institutional regimen of regularly changing service assignments put these incipient personal relationships in a different perspective. Morning rounds give the young resident, in the company of colleagues and the attending physician, a ration of three to five minutes at the patient's bedside. This procedure helps distance everyone from the case. Furthermore, movement from service to service, month after month, systematically prevents residents from staying the course with many of their patients.

The institutional setup subliminally reminds young professionals that they must, above all, refine technical skills. The patient functions as locale for the disease—like a farmhouse on a battleground that acquires interest for the soldier only because of the enemy that may inhabit it. The cumulative impact of the training filters out the personal, not merely the patient as person but the physician as person. The outrageously long hours and exasperating fatigue tell the young resident that no matter what his or her personal state, the job must and will be done. Nervousness, fatigue, faintheartedness, and temptations to self-display burn away, leaving only those skills that define the profession.

At its best, this code, transmitted largely in clinical work, exhibits an aesthetic value. It encourages a proficiency that is quietly eloquent. It conjoins the good with the beautiful. Wasted motion, words, and time fall away. Office life and surgical procedures arrange themselves so as not to impose unduly on the virtuoso's time. Dental technicians do the preparatory work on a series of patients while the dentist moves from chair to chair at just the right moment to perform the work that commands his or her talents. Residents in surgery cut their way in and sew their way out of the patient, leaving the elegant work to the chief surgeon. Professionals subordinate themselves to performance, but the environment similarly must do so. The health care team becomes the instrument in the professional's hands. Attendants, nurses, residents, contributing professionals, anesthesiologists, consultants, pathologists, and the like subordinate themselves to the justifying deed—which, it is hoped, proves to be a beautiful piece of work. A surgery resident describes her experience in the operating room: "I know what it means to call it art—free-standing—almost outside the patient who lies there, draped, the site of the incision alone exposed to view. And when you open up, you don't know what you'll find. No major operation is routine. You have to improvise. An element of ecstasy goes with it. You lose track of time, and, in a sense, also of the patient. You revel in the beauty of the operation, yet you are not wholly divorced from your other roles. To be sure, you divorce the disease from the patient, but it doesn't debase the patient. The surgeon doesn't lose sight of the patient's life. His own self-respect is at stake. He can't let the patient die."

The surgical amphitheater, more than any other site in medicine, symbolizes this emphasis on technical performance, but it shows up elsewhere. As a young resident in internal medicine conceded, attention shifts from the care of patients to the treatment of disease and from the treatment of disease to the treatment of lab tests. The patient and the disease fade away as the physician engages in interventions to bring lab values within acceptable limits. A logical enough shift. Lab tests help to determine the nature and the extent of the trouble and the success of the prescribed remedies. But the physician engages in an essentially aesthetic activity of tuning up, of "sweetenin' the engine," to use Kipling's phrase, a task as far removed from patients per se as the interventions of the ship's engineer or the car mechanic are from the passengers.

The codal ideal of technical performance also provides some basis for group discipline in the medical profession and, further, shapes the form of that discipline. Indeed, the guild deprives few incompetent or unethical doctors of their licenses each year; and it often lacks procedures for retiring the infirm or senescent doctor. But whatever discipline obtains in the profession largely follows the Hemingway pattern. Distinctions develop in professional circles between the truly proficient and the mediocre. The guild will not often act in explicit and overt ways against a deficient member. Rather, colleagues depend on the subtler, unspoken power of the referral system to isolate the mediocre. Few doctors lose their licenses outright. But ostracism, in the form of other doctors discreetly refusing to refer patients to a doctor whose competence they suspect, provides the commonest and most effective form of discipline in the profession today.

Finally, a code provides the modern physician with a basic style of operation that shapes not only his (one thinks chiefly here of the male physician) professional life but his free time. The same pleasure he derives from technical proficiency in his vocation transposes now to his avocations; he develops a Kiplingesque enthusiasm for the machinery of flying, skiing, yachting, or sailing. Because his obligations have placed him daily in the precincts of death, he learns that life may evanesce. Death limits both his life and his free time. It makes sense to live by a code that operates from moment to moment, savoring pleasure in stylish action. Thus his code not only frees him from some of the awkwardness and distress that sentient beings are prey to in the midst of agony, but, when he is momentarily free of the battle, it also provides him with a style and allows him to live, like most warriors who have brushed against death, by the canons of a hedonism that money places within his reach.

The ideal of technical performance deserves criticism from a number of quarters, but many criticisms depend on appeal to other images of the healer. I confine the discussion in this chapter to those criticisms that the concept of *philotechnia* itself generates.

The Greek term *techne* provides the linguistic stem for our modern words "technical" and "technician," but *philotechnia* more directly translates not into the "love of technique" or technology but into the "love of the art." The notion of art differs from technique, technical capacity, or technological resource—as much as Hemingway differs from Kipling. Technology fascinated Kipling. He linked technology with the amplification of imperial power and control and never doubted the beneficence of the results. Kipling more fittingly expressed the technological triumphalism that dominated medicine from the 1930s to the 1980s. Hemingway better highlights that feature of *philotechnia* already identified with the ancient Greeks—a piety toward nature that preserves a sense of the limits of human intervention. Kipling celebrated empire based on a globe-girdling technology that acknowledged no limits to the reach of its power (although Kipling conceded those limits in "Recessional"). But Hemingway's old fisherman, bullfighter, and other heroes overtly acknowledge the limits in their resources. His heroes, whether fisherman, bullfighter, hunter, or soldier, use low-level technology. The equipment employed hardly matches in complexity Kipling's steamship or the modern hospital. Fly rod, handheld gun, or bullfighter's sword resembles the writer's pen and the sculptor's chisel more than the elaborate CAT scanner. In this respect, Hemingway anticipated a recent medical respect for the importance of such humble resources as diet and gymnastics in the improvement of health. *Philotechnia* need not, first and foremost, signify an infatuation with technology but rather a love of the art of healing.

Contemporary medical literature, however, offers little help in understanding the meaning of the phrase "the healer's art." When field practitioners plump for medicine as an art rather than a science, they sound rather apologetic, as though they want to defend a place for themselves and their store of experience in turf largely occupied by their scientifically distinguished colleagues. The latter preside over huge warehouses of knowledge and equipment in tertiary care centers. Alternatively (and somewhat patronizingly), scientists accept healing as an art only in the provisional sense that they cannot yet reduce any and all cases to investigative techniques. Laboratory knowledge still cannot predict every concrete case. If we had fuller knowledge, then the by-guess-and-by-gum, the instinctive surmise, would disappear. Only because of gaps in our scientific knowledge do we need to venture into the intuitive and the imaginative. Thus the art of healing provides but a temporary station on the way to a more perfect science of healing.

The book that presses hardest in favor of the notion of "the healer's art" (Dr. Eric Cassell's volume of that title) nevertheless lacks a chapter or section (or even an index reference to passages) devoted to the meaning of the word "art."[12] Although Dr. Cassell's book offers much material ultimately useful in understanding healing, clearly the profession needs to consider more carefully what it means when it calls healing an art.

The work of art, whether literary or plastic, is both a knowing and a doing: It offers a knowledgeable access to the world, but it also brings into being a new world that was not there before. The classical tradition generally emphasized art as a mode of knowledge; Sophocles' *Oedipus Rex* helps us see into the depths of the holy triad of mother, father, and son with a vividness, concreteness, and universality that ordinary experience does not provide. The romantic tradition, however, emphasized the work of art as a doing; Cézanne's paintings do not merely describe the world as it is, they bring into being a world that hitherto was not there.[13]

The artist's unitary and concrete knowing differs from the scientist's specialized and abstract knowing. The scientist needs to filter out the world in its heterogeneity and deal with purified experience in order to form generalizations about a targeted phenomenon. Therefore the scientist needs a laboratory in which to control variables. He or she does not want the idiosyncrasies of the whole to distract from the part under investigation. Only as abstracted from the concrete world can one know and measure the behavior of the entity in question and anticipate its behavior under similar conditions.

The poet Yeats once complained about the scientific abstraction of the formula $H_2O$, saying that he liked a little seaweed in his definition of water. He slyly underlined thereby the poet's (and the human) preference for the concrete, full-bodied, and heterogeneous over abstract formula. However heterogeneous it may be, the artist gives access to an organized, not a disorganized, world and offers a unitary and ordered field of vision. Just so, Hemingway's heroes function as artists. The old man, pursuing the marlin, closely scans his world: the patterns of the tide, the weather, the condition of his boat, his equipment, his body, the likely limits of his endurance, the behavior of the fish on which the marlin might feed, and the sharks that lie in wait after the catch. The fisherman, like the artist, brings into view a concrete universe that one sees fully only with one's eyes.

But art also does something. The artist brings into existence a concrete universe that would not be there apart from the creative act. Romanticists emphasized the creative, as opposed to the cognitive, aspect of the work of art. They celebrated the demiurgic power whereby the artist pulled worlds into being superior in some respects to the one that we know.[14] W. H. Auden, although no romantic, conceded two levels of praise for the work of art. Writer A prompts us to say: He has perfectly described the world of the drugstore; Writer B leads us to say: He has given us a drugstore the likes of which we have not seen before. And yet Writer B does not altogether disconnect us from or vanquish the ordinary world: He engages in a creative reconstruction that, while catching our eye, helps us also to see the world of the drugstore in a new light.

Healing, as an art, displays both a cognitive and a creative aspect. The cognitive component in the healing process—both diagnostic and prognostic—acts partly as science but partly as art. As science, it requires specialized and abstract investigatory work. Each medical specialty rests on its peculiar knowledge base; it relies on a series of indicators that signal the presence of diseases that its technical interventions affect; it maintains these interventions at the ready. This specialized knowledge and activity systematically abstract from the patient as a whole, by ignoring the technically irrelevant.

But the cognitive component of healing includes a further element. The healer not only must attempt to cure disease but must address the illness of which the disease forms but a part. As Dr. Cassell has put it, "Disease . . . is something an organ has; illness is something a man has."[15] The host may be incidental to the disease (sometimes, not always), but the host is rarely incidental to the state of illness. The healer who would make whole distracted patients, whose illness has, according to Dr. Cassell's report, disconnected them from their world, weakened their self- and body-confidence, and imposed on them a loss of self-control—such a healer cannot rest content with a specialized and abstract knowledge of disease, as much as that may contribute to the enterprise. The healer looks at the whole patient, the full range of somatic and psychic structures disrupted by disease. Such a knowledge must, ultimately, unite and specify, situating the disease in a particular person and in his or her idiosyncratic social history. The knowledge resembles more the coordinations of an experienced fisherman scanning the sea or a hunter wary in the woods or a cook fully experienced in the kitchen than it resembles the reductions of a case to a general law.

Finally, of course, the healer's knowing aims at doing. The healer's art creates as well as knows, and the constructive activity in which the healer engages includes more than curing disease. The fully rounded work of healing reconnects the patient with the world and recovers his or her self-control and self-confidence. The treatment plan at its best offers a coherent, total program for as much recovery as a particular patient can achieve under the circumstances. Preventive medicine and chronic care, just as much as acute and rehabilitative medicine, require artistic intervention. Admittedly, such care has its routines, techniques, and tricks. No art form lacks its conventions. But these activities ultimately aim to reorder comprehensively a human life. That work, in the nature of the case, must unite and specify.

Finally, the physician cannot successfully enact a program of preventive, rehabilitative, and chronic care without the patient's cooperation. The reconstruction of habits requires that the patient personally must accept some responsibility for a unitary, comprehensive, and concrete governance of his or her life and health. Studies, however, have shown that patients do not readily accept this responsibility unless they, to some degree, share the physician's knowledge and understanding. In effect, the physician cannot engage in artistic reconstruction unless the patient personally internalizes the need to resculpt his or her life. At that point, the image of the physician as technician and artist shifts into the images of the physician as covenanter and teacher.

## Chapter Four

# The Physician's Covenant

Ernest Hemingway's works illuminate a professional ethic that prizes technique as a shield against ties. William Faulkner's novels and stories create a bonded world. Faulkner's characters take their bearing from a promissory event. He usually wrote about the ties of marriage and the family, the bond between the races and the generations, or the primordial tie to the land. Hemingway and Faulkner both wrote about men who kill animals; Hemingway used such deaths as climaxes to end a poem ("and then it was over"); Faulkner used them as a sacrifice to establish a covenant, as in "Delta Autumn":

> I slew you; my bearing must not shame your quitting life. My conduct forever onward must become your death.[1]

Isaac McCaslin made this unspoken promise as he killed his first deer under the tutelage of old Sam Fathers, the Indian who taught him to hunt. Some seventy years later, old Isaac McCaslin still returns annually to that sacred place where, as a boy, he learned to hunt. During the annual trek back into the delta, he recovers that moment, seven decades ago, when he first slew his deer, what Faulkner calls else-where the "binding instant":

> ... and the gun leveled rapidly without haste and crashed and he walked to the buck lying still in the shape of that magnificent speed and bled it with Sam's knife and Sam dipped his hands into hot blood and marked his forehead forever.[2]

The event alters his being: It binds and judges the rest of his life, whatever its content. From then on, just as the marked Jew, the errant, harassed, and estranged Jew, recovers through ritual renewal the covenant of the exodus and Mount Sinai, Isaac returns to the delta every autumn to renew the hunt and to suffer there his own renewal despite the alienation he has subsequently known across a lifetime.

This promissory event shapes his future morally as well as ritually. The covenant details duties that give specific content to the future, while enjoining a comprehensive fidelity that extends beyond particulars to unforeseen and unforeseeable contingencies. The hunter's specific duties in this case include learning how to use a rifle to bring down game and a knife to kill. More broadly, he must also protect the species on which the hunt depends; this obligation demands that he protect the doe and the wilderness so crucial to its flourishing. Metaphorically, the covenant broadens still further to enjoin fitting ways to use land and respect for the human community that uses it. (In the story, Faulkner nicely juxtaposes obligations to the nonhuman and the human worlds through the metaphor of the doe. A faithless hunter violates covenantal fidelity not only by killing a doe but by abandoning a black woman who has borne his child.) The <u>duty to protect the weak and the vulnerable</u> eventually expands into a comprehensive fidelity that exceeds specification. It includes the contingent needs of others that the original covenant could not specifically anticipate.

Finally, a future-shaping covenant centers on a promise, but it does not begin with that <u>promise</u>. It begins, still earlier, with what the initiate <u>received and assumed as a gift</u>:

> He seemed to see the two of them—himself and the wilderness as coevals, his own span as a hunter, a woodsman not contemporary with his first breath but transmitted to him, assumed by him gladly, humbly, with joy and pride, from that old Major de Spain and that old Sam Fathers who had taught him how to hunt.[3]

The gifts are several: the wilderness and its game, but also the gift of instruction by mentors, who have taught him how to respect the wilderness and to hunt. These <u>gifts precede the promise</u>—just as the gifts of courtship precede a marriage vow, and, in the Scriptures of Israel, the exodus precedes Mount Sinai. The Jews bind themselves to God at Mount Sinai as those who have already received an astonishing gift, the deliverance from Egypt. A covenantal ethic positions human givers in the context of a primordial act of receiving a gift not wholly deserved, which they can only assume gratefully. God tells the Israelites: When you harvest your crops, leave some for the sojourner. For you were once sojourners in Egypt. Givers themselves receive. Benefactors ultimately benefit.

The biblical understanding of covenant defines the world about which Faulkner writes. The Scriptures of ancient Israel are littered with such covenants and covenantal duties: between men and women (the covenant of marriage), between men and men (the covenants of friendship), between nations (treaties and covenants of conquest), between a people and the stranger in the midst (duties to the sojourner), and between the generations (the transmission of a blessing, with its filial duties). But these secondary covenants derive from and reflect imperfectly that singular covenant that embraces all others, the covenant of the people with God.

The primary religious covenant includes the aforementioned elements: first, an original gift between the soon-to-be covenanted partners (the deliverance of the people from Egypt); second, a promise based on the original or anticipated gift (the vows at Mount Sinai). These two aspects of covenant, taken together, alter the being of the covenanted people (God "marks the forehead" of the Jews forever) so that fidelity to the covenant defines their subsequent life. Third, the covenanted people accept an inclusive set of ritual and moral obligations by which they will live. These commands are both specific enough to make the future duties of Israel concrete (e.g., the dietary laws and laws governing protection of the weak), yet summary enough (e.g., "Love the Lord thy God with all thy heart . . .") to require a fidelity to the intent as well as to the letter.

This brief summary of the structural features of a covenantal ethic does not yet suggest how it would work out in a professional setting—except to contrast starkly with an ethic that eschews ties and commitments. Just how it grounds obligations to patients, colleagues, the profession, and the wider society unfolds in due course as we compare the ethic with an ideal and a mechanism that in some particulars it resembles: the philanthropic ideal enshrined in the written codes of the profession and the marketplace mechanism of contractual agreements.

## The Hippocratic Oath

Although the notion of covenant originates and develops primarily in the biblical tradition, a covenantal ingredient also figures in the classical physician's oath. The Hippocratic Oath includes three parts: first, codal duties to patients; second, covenantal obligations to one's teacher and his family; and, third, the setting of both in the context of an oath to the gods.

The physician's duties to his patients, as noted earlier, include a series of absolute prohibitions and positive injunctions largely philanthropic in their origin (and partly technical in their content). The second set of obligations, directed to the physician's teacher, his teacher's children, and his own, require him to accept full filial responsibilities for his adoptive father's personal and financial welfare and to transmit without fee his art and knowledge to the teacher's progeny and his own and to other pupils, but only those others who take the oath according to medical law. The setting and the spirit of the second set of obligations differ from those of the first.

In his study of the Hippocratic Oath, the historian Ludwig Edelstein characterizes those duties that a physician undertakes toward patients as an ethical code and those assumed toward the professional guild (one's teachers) as a covenant. Edelstein traces this difference to the Pythagorean convention of adopting the student by oath into the "family" of the teacher.[4]

In my judgment, the fact of indebtedness constitutes the chief reason for using the term "covenant."

The word conveniently describes the distinctive obligations to one's teacher. Physicians undertake duties to their patients, but they *owe something* to their teachers. They have received goods and services for which they owe their filial services. Toward their patients, they function as benefactors, but toward their teachers, they relate as beneficiaries. This responsiveness to gift characterizes a covenant. Both the Hammurabic Code and the Mosaic law state those laws and statutes that will shape their respective civilizations; but the biblical covenant differs from the Hammurabic and other codes. It places the moral duties of the people in the all-important context of a divine gift of deliverance. When the people of Israel promise to obey God, they respond to goods already received. Analogously, in the Hippocratic Oath, the physician undertakes obligations to the teacher and the teacher's progeny out of gratitude for services already rendered. The modern practice of medicine has tended to reinforce this ancient distinction between code and covenant and has opted for code as the ruling ideal in relationships to patients, but not with altogether favorable consequences for the moral health of the profession.

The countless exchanges between colleagues— referrals, favors, personal confidences, tips, training, consultations, and collaborative work on cases— strengthen, amplify, and intensify this ancient bond with the teacher (colleague). Loyalty to colleagues grows as a response to gifts already received and to those anticipated. Rules governing behavior toward patients have a different ring to them from that fealty which physicians owe their colleagues. The medical codes do not interpret duties to patients as a partly responsive act for gifts and services received. This element of covenantal indebtedness does not figure in the interpretation of professional duties to patients from obligations of the Hippocratic Oath to the modern codes of the AMA.

The Hippocratic Oath, of course, includes a third element: a vow, or religious oath proper, directed to the gods. "I swear by Apollo Physician, and Asclepius and Hygeia, and Panaceia and all the gods and goddesses, making them my witnesses, that I will fulfill according to my ability and judgment this oath and this covenant."[5] A religious reference appears again in the statement of duties to the patient: "In purity and holiness I will guard my life and my art." And the promise maker finally petitions: "If I fulfill this oath and do not violate it, may it be granted to me to enjoy life and art . . .; if I transgress it and swear falsely, may the opposite of all this be My lot."[6]

This religious oath, in the literal sense of the term, made a "professional" out of the man who subscribed to it. He professed or testified thereby to the power of healing, which his duties to his patients and his obligations to his teacher made specific. Swearing by Apollo and Asclepius affirmed the ontological root of his life. He professed, in effect, those powers that altered his own state of being. Henceforth he was a professional, a professor of healing.

This third element in the Hippocratic Oath, so interpreted, expands the covenant to refer not simply to a limited indebtedness to one's teachers but also, more broadly, to those transcendent powers on which healing depends. The religious oath partly resembled a covenant in that the physician made a promise that referred to the gods from whose power the profession of healing ultimately derives. To this degree, it put the physician in the position of a recipient. This religious promise supported that secondary promise that the physician made to care for his teacher and to fulfill his duties to his patients.

Yet in two important respects, the vow itself differs from a biblical covenant: It offers no prefatory statement about the actions of the divine to which the human promise responds; and its form deemphasizes the responsive nature of the physician's action, for he swears *by* the gods instead of promises to the gods to fulfill his professional duties. His promise by the gods simply gives gravity and shape to the details of the oath.

Detached altogether from this religious vow, both the Hippocratic Oath and the profession that it helped to shape move further toward a purely codal definition of duties to patients. These duties, as transmitted in a clinical setting, largely prize the ideal of technical efficiency. But, as engraved in the written tablets of the profession, they elevate into the compensatory and ultimately pretentious ideal of philanthropy.

## Philanthropy versus Covenantal Indebtedness

The philanthropic ideal of service to humankind, inscribed in the written codes, cannot be faulted for its material content. It succumbs, however, to what might be called the conceit of philanthropy when it assumes that the professional's commitment to patients is a wholly gratuitous rather than a responsive act. The codes acknowledge, in modern times, neither an indebtedness to a transcendent source nor the physician's substantial indebtedness to the community. As a result, the odor of condescension taints the documents. The American code of 1847, for example, asserts that the patients' duties derive from what they have received from their doctors:

The members of the medical profession, upon whom is enjoined the performance of so many important and arduous duties, toward the community, and who are required to make so many sacrifices of comfort, ease, and health, for the welfare of those who avail themselves of their services, certainly have a right to expect and require that their patients should entertain a just sense of the duties which they owe to their medical attendants.[7]

In like manner, the section "Obligations of the Public to Physicians" emphasizes those many gifts and services that the public has received from, and that create its indebtedness to, the medical profession.

The benefits accruing to the public, directly and indirectly, from the active and unwearied beneficiaries of the profession, are so numerous and important that physicians are justly entitled to the utmost consideration and respect from the community.[8]

But turning to the preamble on the physician's duties to the patient and the public, we find no corresponding section of the code of 1847 (or 1957) that acknowledges, or even partly derives, physicians' duties from those gifts and services that they have received from the community. Thus the code offers the picture of a relatively self-sufficient monad, who out of the nobility and generosity of his disposition and the gratuitously accepted conscience of his profession has taken on himself the noble life of service. The false posturing in all this is blurted out in one of the opening sections of the 1847 code. Physicians "should study, also, in their deportment so as to unite tenderness with firmness, and condescension with authority, so as to inspire the minds of their patients with gratitude, respect, and confidence."[9]

Significantly, the code shifts its terms, depending on the direction in which it moves. It refers not to the "Obligations of Patients to Their Physicians" but the "Duties of Physicians to Their Patients." The shift from "Obligations" to "Duties" may seem slight, but, in fact, it reveals a differing source and intensity to moral claim. "Obligation" has the same root as the words "ligament" and "religion"; it emphasizes a bind, a bond, a tie. The AMA viewed the patient and public as bound and indebted to the profession for its services but viewed the profession as accepting *duties* to the patient and public out of a noble conscience rather than a reciprocal sense of indebtedness.

The profession parodies God not so much because it exercises power of life and death over others, but because it does not really think of itself as beholden, even partially, to anyone for those duties to patients that it lays on itself. The profession claims the godlike power to draw its life from itself alone and to act wholly gratuitously.

In fact, however, the physician owes a very considerable debt to the community. The original Hippocratic Oath adumbrates the first of these. The physician owes someone or some group for his or her education. In ancient times, this led to a special sense of covenantal obligation to one's teacher. Under the conditions of modern medical education, the profession owes obligations both substantial (far exceeding the social investment in the training of any other professional) and widely distributed (including not only teachers but those public monies that provide for medical education, the teaching hospital, and massive research into disease).

Because many more qualified candidates apply to medical school than can be admitted and because, until recently, the society needed many more doctors than the schools could train, physicians incur a second order of indebtedness for the privilege of practice that has almost arbitrarily come their way. Although the 1847 code refers to the "privileges" of being a doctor, it does not specify the social origins of those privileges. Third, and not surprisingly, the codes do not refer to that extraordinary social largesse that befalls the physician, in payment for services, especially in a society suffering from a limitless fear of death and, until recently, a limited supply of personnel. Furthermore, the codes do not concede the indebtedness of the physician to those patients who have offered themselves as subjects for experimentation or as teaching material (either in teaching hospitals or in the early years of practice). Early practice includes, after all, the element of increased risk for patients who lay their bodies on the line as the apprentice doctor practices on them. The pun in the word "practice" but reflects the inevitable social price of training.

Judah Folkman, M.D., in a class day address to young graduates at Harvard Medical School, eloquently acknowledged this indebtedness to the patient, which, he suggests, physicians must repay, much "like tithing." Such *pro bono publico* work might take various forms: a willingness to see Medicaid patients; attending continuing education courses and taking recertification examinations; carrying out investigation or researach; or perhaps even doing volunteer work for national or philanthropic services.[10]

Physicians not only owe their patients for a start in their careers but remain unceasingly in their debt. The power and authority that mature professionals exude somewhat obscure this reciprocity of need. They seem self-sufficient virtuosos whose life derives from their competence, whereas others appear before them in their indigence, their illness, their crimes, or their ignorance, for which the professional, as doctor, lawyer, or teacher, offers remedy.

In fact, however, a reciprocity of giving and receiving nourishes the professional relationship. The professional does not function as benefactor alone but also as beneficiary. In teaching, for example, students need a teacher, but the teacher also needs students. They provide the teacher with a regular occasion and forum in which to work out what he or she has to say and to rediscover the subject afresh through the discipline of sharing it with others. Likewise, the doctor needs patients. No one can watch a physician nervously approach retirement without realizing how much the doctor has needed the patients to be himself or herself.

A covenantal ethic helps acknowledge this context of need and indebtedness in which professionals undertake and discharge their duties. It also relieves professionals of the temptation and pressure to pretend that they are demigods exempt from human exigency. In addition to the specific ways in which they owe their patients, professionals stand unceasingly exigent and needy before God. The derivation of the notion of professional covenant from a divine-human covenant should not seduce us into slotting healers (and other professionals) into the position of God. God is not to humankind as the healer is to his or her patients. Despite all flattering impressions to the contrary, professionals undertake their responsibilities not as godly benefactors but as those who, first and foremost, benefit. The human activities of healing, teaching, parenting, and the like, do not create—that is God's work—but, from beginning to end, respond. Only within a fundamental responsiveness do professionals undertake their secondary little initiatives on behalf of others.

## Contract or Covenant

While criticizing the ideal of philanthropy, I have emphasized the elements of exchange and reciprocity that mark the professional relationship. Should we therefore eliminate the element of the gratuitous in professional ethics? Do physicians merely respond to the social investment in their training, the fees paid for their services, and the terms of an agreement drawn up between themselves and their patients, the element of the gratuitous altogether disappearing?

Does covenant simply act as a commercial contract in which two parties calculate their respective best interests and agree on some joint project from which both derive roughly equivalent benefits for good contributed by each? If so, covenantal ethics would support those theorists who would interpret the doctor-patient relationship as a legal agreement and assimilate medical ethics to medical law.

The notion of the physician as contractor has obvious appeal. First, it breaks with more authoritarian models (such as parent or priest). It emphasizes informed consent rather than blind trust; it encourages respect for the dignity of the patient, who does not, because of illness, forfeit autonomy as a human being; it also encourages specifying rights, duties, conditions, and qualifications that limit the contract.

In effect, it establishes some symmetry and mutuality in the relationship between doctor and patient as they exchange information and reach an agreement, tacit or explicit, to exchange goods (money for services).

Second, a contract provides for the legal enforcement of terms on both parties and thus offers each some protection and recourse under the law to make the other accountable under the contract.

Finally, a contract does not rely on the pose of philanthropy or condescend as "charity." It frankly presupposes that self-interest primarily governs people. When two parties enter into a contract, they do so because each cuts a deal that serves his or her own advantage. Self-interest motivates not only private contracts but also that primordial contract in and through which the state came into being. So argued the contractarians of the seventeenth and eighteenth centuries. The state does not derive from some heroic act of sacrifice by gods or men. Rather men and women "left" the state of nature and entered into the political contract because each served thereby his or her own advantage. They surrendered some liberty and property to the state to escape the evils that would beset them individually apart from the state's protection. The state arises as a defensive reaction, on behalf of self-interest, against the threat of murder, anarchy, theft, and other forms of the threat of violent death.

Subsequent enthusiasts about the social instrument of contracts[11] have measured human progress by the degree to which a society bases its life on contracts rather than on status. By this measure, the ancient Romans made the most striking progress when they used commercial contracts where custom previously ruled. The modern bourgeoisie extended the use of contracts still further into economics and politics and even into religion with the free-church emphasis on voluntary choice rather than received religious traditions. Some educators today have used the device of contracts in the classroom (as they encourage students and teachers to reach explicit agreements about units of work for levels of grade). More recently, some liberationists would extend it into marriage; and still others would prefer to see it define the professional relationship. The movement, on the whole, intends to laicize authority, legalize relationships, activate self-interest, and encourage collaboration.

Some of these aims of the contractualists appeal strongly, but it would be unfortunate if professional ethics folded into a commercial contract alone. First, the notion of contract suppresses the element of gift in human relationships. Earlier I verged on denying the importance of this ingredient in professional relationships when I criticized the medical profession for its conceit of philanthropy, its self-interpretation as the great giver. In fact, I do not object to the notion of gift but to the moral pretension of professionals who see themselves as givers alone.

The contractualist approach tends to reduce professional obligation to self-interested minimalism, quid pro quo. Do no more for your patients than what the contract calls for: specified services for established fees. A commercial contract may be a fitting instrument in the purchase of an appliance, a house, or services that can be specified fully in advance of delivery. A legally enforceable agreement in professional transactions may also protect the patient or client against the physician or lawyer whose services fall below a minimal standard. But reducing duties to the specifics of a contract alone fails to honor the full scope of professional obligation.

Professionals in the so-called helping professions serve unpredictable needs. The professional deals with the sickness, ills, crimes, needs, and tragedies of humankind. No contract can exhaustively specify in advance for each patient or client. The professions must be ready to cope with the contingent and the unexpected. Calls on services may exceed those needs anticipated in a contract or the compensation available in a given case. Services moreover are more likely to achieve the desired therapeutic result if they come in the context of a relationship that the patient or client can really trust.

Contract and covenant, materially considered, appear to be first cousins; they both include an agreement and an exchange between parties. But in spirit, contract and covenant differ markedly. Contracts are external; covenants are internal to the parties involved. We sign contracts to discharge them expediently. Covenants cut deeper into personal identity. A contract has a limited duration, but the religious covenant imposes change on all moments. A mechanic can act under a contract, and then, when not fixing a piston, act without regard to the contract; but a covenantal people acts under covenant while eating, sleeping, working, praying, cheating, healing, or blundering.

Paul remarks, in effect: When you eat, eat to the glory of God, and when you fast, fast to the glory of God, and when you marry, marry to the glory of God, and when you abstain, abstain to the glory of God (1 Corinthians 10). Initiation into a profession means, in effect, that the physician is a healer when healing and when sleeping, when practicing and when malpracticing. In the modern world, this dedication has deteriorated into the macho ethic of residency training, particularly in surgery: twelve hours a day, six days a week, and night service every other night, on and off for five years. But such training (despite its morally and professionally dubious aspects) does bespeak a deep claim on the person's identity.

Covenants also have a gratuitous, growing edge to them that springs from this ontological change and builds relationships. No one has put this contrasting feature of a contract and a covenant better than Faulkner in his comic novel *Intruder in the Dust*.

At the outset of the novel, a white boy, hunting with young blacks, falls into a creek on a cold winter day. While thrashing about in the icy water, he feels a long pole jab at his body and hears a commanding black voice say, "Boy, grab hold." After the boy clambers out of the river, Lucas Beauchamp, a proud, older black man, brings him shivering to his house, where Mrs. Beauchamp takes care of him. She takes off his wet clothes and wraps him in "Negro blankets," feeds him "Negro food," and warms him by the fire.

When his clothes dry, the boy dresses to go, but, uneasy about his debt to Lucas, he reaches into his pocket for some coins and offers 70 cents compensation for Beauchamp's help. Lucas rejects the money firmly and commands the two black boys to pick up the coins from the floor where they have fallen and to return them to the white boy, who thus fails in his effort to get rid of his feeling of indebtedness.

Shortly thereafter, still uneasy about the episode at the river and his frustrated effort to pay off Lucas for his help, the boy buys some imitation silk for Lucas's wife and gets his black friend to deliver it. Now he feels better. But a few days later, the white boy goes to his own backdoor stoop only to find a jug of molasses that Lucas has left for him. The gift puts him back where he started, again beholden to the black man.

Several months later, the boy passes Lucas on the street and scans his face closely, wondering whether the black man remembers the incident between them—a little like the high school boy who spies the girl in the hall the morning after and reads her face to see what registers from the evening before. He can't be sure. Four years pass, and town authorities falsely accuse Lucas of murdering a white man. They take him to the jailhouse, where a crowd gathers to watch. The boy goes early, watches the proceedings, and ponders whether the old man remembers their past encounter. Just as Lucas is about to enter the jailhouse, he wheels and points his long arm in the direction of the boy and says, "Boy, I want to see you." The boy obeys and visits Lucas in the jailhouse, and eventually he and his aunt succeed in proving Lucas's innocence.

Faulkner's story serves as a parable for the relationship of whites to blacks in the South. Black people have labored in white people's fields, built and cared for their houses, fed, clothed, and nurtured their children. In accepting these labors, the whites have received their life and substance from the blacks over and over again. But they resist this involvement and try to pay off the blacks with a few marketplace coins. They try to define their relationship as transient and external, to be managed at arm's length.

For better or for worse, blacks and whites in this country share a common life and destiny. They cannot resolve the problem between them until they accept the covenant that the original receipt of labor entails.

The story emphasizes the donative element in the upbuilding and nourishing of covenant—whether the covenant of marriage, friendship, or professional relationship. Quid pro quo characterizes a commercial transaction, but covenantally, each partner must serve and draw on the deeper reserves of the other. Contractual exchanges of buying and selling can expand into further episodes of giving and receiving, but then they deepen toward a covenantal bond.

This donative element should infuse not only the healer's care of the patient but also other aspects of health care. In his fascinating study *The Gift Relationship*, the late economist Richard M. Titmuss compared the voluntary British system of obtaining blood with the American system, which relies heavily on buying blood.[12] The British system obtains more and better blood without exploiting the indigent, which the American system has condoned and which our courts encouraged when they refused to exempt nonprofit blood banks from the antitrust laws. By court definition, blood exchange becomes a commercial transaction in the United States. Titmuss extended his critique beyond the limited subject of human blood to general social policy by offering a sober comment on the increased commercialism of American medicine (and American society at large). Recent court decisions have tended to shift more and more professional services into the category of commodity transactions, with negative consequences—Titmuss believed—for health care delivery systems. Quite apart from court decisions, physicians have contributed to this commercialization of medicine by their strong support for a fee-for-service system of compensation, as opposed to systems that rely on salaried professionals. A piece-work payment system tends to reduce the professional transaction even further in the direction of closely calibrated, self-interested exchange.

The minimalism that a purely contractualist understanding of the professional relationship encourages produces a professional too grudging, too calculating, too lacking in spontaneity, too quickly exhausted to go the second mile with patients along the road of their distress.

Contract medicine not only encourages minimalism; it also provokes a peculiar maximalism, "defensive medicine." Under the pressure of the fear of disease and death, patients often push for the maximum in tests and procedures, and physicians often yield to (or exploit) these fears, because they fear malpractice suits. Paradoxically, contractualism tempts the doctor simultaneously to do too little and too much for the patient—too little in that one extends oneself only to the limits the contract specifies, and too much in that one orders procedures that are useful in pampering the patient and protecting oneself, even though the patient's condition does not demand them. The emphasis on self-interest in contractual decisions provides the link between these apparently contradictory strategies of too little and too much. The element of gratuitous service vanishes.

Given its emphasis on self-interest, a contractualist ethic must rely too heavily on several external restraints to keep the supplier of services within moral limits. In commerce, consumers presumably protect themselves by acquiring knowledge about the products they purchase. Insofar as contract medicine encourages increased knowledge on the part of the patient, well and good. But relying exclusively on the injunction "Let the buyer beware" to keep the seller within bounds does not work. A latent antinomianism underlies this conventional marketplace control. It suggests that the seller has few obligations above and beyond those that the knowledge or skepticism of the buyer enforces. This marketplace mechanism alone will not suffice in medical practice. The physician's knowledge so exceeds that of the patient that the patient's knowledgeability alone will not satisfactorily constrain the physician's behavior. One must, at least in part, cultivate some internal fiduciary checks that physicians (and their guilds) will honor.

The consumer's freedom to shop and choose among various vendors provides another self-regulating mechanism in the traditional contractual relationship. Certainly this freedom of choice needs expansion by the better distribution of physicians, the provision of alternative delivery systems, and the proper development of paramedical personnel. However, the crises under which many patients press for medical services do not always provide them with the leisure or calm required for discretionary judgment. Thus normal marketplace controls will never wholly protect the consumer in dealings with the physician.

Finally, the reduction of ethics to contractualism alone fails to judge the more powerful of the two parties (the professional) by transcendent standards. Normally conceived, ethics establishes rights and duties that transcend the particulars of a given agreement. The standards then measure the justice of any specific contract. If, however, such rights and duties inhere only in the contract, then a patient or client might legitimately waive his or her rights. The contract determines only what is required, not necessarily what is just. That arrangement simply augments the power of the more preponderant of the two bargainers. A contract cannot demand an illegal act and should not allow an unethical act. Professional ethics should not permit a professional to persuade his or her patient to waive rights that transcend the particulars of their agreement.

As opposed to a marketplace contractualist ethic, the biblical notion of covenant obliges the more pow-

erful to accept some responsibility for the more vulnerable and powerless of the two partners. It does not
permit a free rein to self-interest, subject only to the
capacity of the weaker partner to protect himself or
herself through knowledge, shrewdness, and purchasing power. Faulkner's novels have highlighted this
feature of covenantal ethics. The background for
Faulkner's sense of covenant lies in Scripture: The
Mount Sinai covenant requires the Israelites to accept
responsibility for the widow, the orphan, the stranger,
and the poor in their midst. Still earlier, the covenant
with Noah set forth a responsibility for the nonhuman
creation. And Jesus later insisted that God will measure his people by their treatment of the sick, the
imprisoned, the hungry, and the thirsty; God joins
himself to the needy and makes their cause his own.
Contractualism, on the contrary, builds few constraints on action other than those that prudent self-
interest and explicit legislation impose.

Robert Veatch, in *A Theory of Medical Ethics*,[13] has
responded to the criticisms I have directed against the
notion of contract as a basis for medical ethics by dis-
tinguishing between a commercial contract and a primordial social contract that provides a transcendent
standard of moral judgment.[14] Veatch largely draws his
view of the latter, not from the earlier contractarian
theorists Hobbes and Locke, but from a conflation of
John Rawls's theory of justice[15] and Roderick Firth's
theory of the ideal observer.[16] Thereby Veatch tries to
rescue the idea of contract from the cruder features of
self-interest and recommend it as a kind of secular
equivalent to the religious notion of covenant.[17]
Purged of crude self-interest, the notion of contract
provides some protection for the powerless. Rawls,
for example, invites us to play a game whereby we

withdraw from the world as we know it, including knowledge of our peculiar slot in life—as doctor, lawyer, car washer, or unemployed person—and assume an imaginary "original position" of ignorance in which we do not yet know our actual power, talents, or fate. Given this veil of ignorance, all prudently self-interested persons, Rawls argues, will agree to a fundamental social contract that will insist on equality of treatment for all participants (excepting those inequalities that work to the advantage of the least advantaged). Thus a social contract emerges—based on rational self-interest—that protects the interest of all, including the poor. Such principles of fairness ought to govern the fundamental institutions of the land, including, Veatch believes, the professional relationship. Social contract theory thus offers a secular surrogate for covenant, free of the crass forms of self-interest that sully marketplace contracts. Reason, rather than religious tradition, seems to arrive at a transcendent standard of judgment that protects the powerless.

Such contractarianism fails at two points. First, its conception of humankind is insufficiently communal. Its original appeal to an isolated self-interest generates, to be sure, principles of fairness, but self-interest alone does not suffice to carry over those principles from a fictitious original position into the actual world. It may well be that an isolated self—under the conditions of ignorance about its own position in the lottery of life—would self-protectively choose social principles of fair distribution. But if it carries that self-interest and nothing more over into the actual world, what would give the self the motivation not to compromise the rules of the game whenever those rules no longer served its wants and interests? Does not the original self require a more communal sense of humankind, a more spacious sense of the common good, in order to sustain its commitment to a principle of fair distribution under the pressured conditions of existence?

Second, recent contractarianism does not reckon with the full destructive force of the actual world, which tempts us to abandon the ideal of rational self-interest.[18] We drive hard bargains and give the needy short shrift because we find ourselves not in an original position of ignorance but in the thick of the race—beleaguered by competitors, creditors, deadlines, demanding patients, and threats of disaster, disease, and death. Imagining an ideal state does not curb the beast of self-interest within us or the dread on which it feeds: the fear that our competitors will do us in or that we will slide into the vortex of decay and death with the powerless if we get too close to them. Aggressive self-interest rules us because it seems to answer the threat of death. It appeals by virtue of its apparent metaphysical realism.

Ultimately the steadfast commitment to protect, nourish, and heal the needy will falter unless we have some resource for reckoning with the harsh world of which needy people so palpably remind us, with the threat of poverty, failure, and death. A steadfast commitment to the needy and their cause requires more than an appeal to an ideal of rational self-interest abstracted from the world that we know. It requires placing that harsh world in the context of yet another world, more powerful, plausible, and gripping, that both deals with the sting of suffering and death and makes it possible, tolerable, imperative, and inviting for us to deal with the needy (and our own needs) in a better way. To describe contract as a secular version of covenant reduces religion to a matter of dispensable trimming. It fails to reckon with religion in its metaphysical substance, that is, its attempt in faith to delineate, in ritual to re-present, and in ethics to honor the real.

This discussion of contract and covenant, then, forces a return to the world that the biblical covenant presents as it attempts to deal with the sting of disease, suffering, and death. Without discussion of that threat, a covenantal imperative to serve the needy will seem just as marginal to the real world as the moral ideal of rational self-interest.[19]

## Covenant in the Christian Setting

The healer nurtured in the Christian understanding of covenant affirms the Holy of Holies as creative, nurturant, and donative rather than destructive. This affirmation does not deny the reality of disease, pain, suffering, and death but puts them in the setting of a power that persists and endures in the very midst of them. God ultimately encompasses suffering and death; they are *real* but not *ultimate*; they do not speak the last word about the human condition. The Christian sees in Jesus an event that does not eliminate suffering and death (How could it? The Savior himself experienced the full range of human need; he suffered under Pontius Pilate, was crucified, dead, and buried) but instead exposes destructive power in its final impotence to separate men and women from God.

The term "new covenant" describes the peculiar gift of this self-expending love, its human reception, and promissory ties to it. In laying down his own life, Jesus takes up death itself into the power of donative love. He himself gives and receives in the midst of his own dying and allows others to participate in the selfsame power. This love does not extricate men and women from the arena of human need, suffering, and death, but relieves this arena of its terror. The covenant in Christ, in effect, locates the self, the beleaguered, fearful self, within the dynamics of giving and receiving—gift love and need love—and thus allows the Christian to sit loose to the world: to enter the world without panicking before it or getting mired in it. The covenant deepens ties to the world precisely because it has lightened them. The bond to the world and the patient becomes bearable because, strictly speaking, the covenanted cannot take the ideals and terrors of the ordinary world with ultimate seriousness. The covenantal setting frees us from the need to avoid ties to the perishing. The dying—and we ourselves in the midst of them—are no longer marked by the absence of God. That nonchalance of which the apostle Paul speaks in Romans provides the setting for a truly serious-lighthearted medical practice.

> Neither death, nor life, nor angels, nor principalities, nor things present, nor things to come, nor powers, nor height, nor depth, nor anything else in all creation, will be able to separate us from the love of God. (Rom. 8:38–39)

That primordial tie makes other ties bearable.

Detached from this setting, however, the ideals of technical proficiency, philanthropy, and contract tend to deteriorate into devices whereby healers, beset by pain, pettiness, and suffering, shield themselves from patients and their perishing life. Professionals who prize technique alone find in their technique a protection against the terrible disorder of war, disease, and death and their emotional reaction to it. The philanthropist solves the problem of neediness by adopting the pose of the self-sufficient giver who extends a hand while figuring out how to wriggle free. Philanthropy offers a doctrine of love without ties. It deteriorates into condescension, not because philanthropists harbor a conviction of their ultimate superiority to petitioners, but because they fear that they will drown in a sea of need if they step down from their promontory. Contractors, similarly, seek to solve the problem of perishing by keeping their commitments limited—so much piecework for so much pay, whether directly or indirectly compensated under a third-party payment system. Contractors thus dart in and out of the patient's world of need, shoring up their own life through the transaction of selling. Contractors guard their own interest, carefully specifying the precise amount of time and service for sale. Thus code, philanthropy, and contract, within the context of death, are all devices for evading ties. All have in common a fear of perishing, of drowning in the plight of the other. Ties suck one down into the vortex of death. To call contract, or any other of these devices, merely a secular version of covenant overlooks the important question of metaphysical setting.

Covenantal ethics, despite its advantages over the ideal of philanthropy and the legal instrument of contract, generates difficulties that only a setting in the transcendent resolves. As opposed to the ideal of philanthropy that pretends to wholly gratuitous altruism, covenantal ethics is responsive. As opposed to the instrument of contract that presupposes agreement reached on the basis of self-interest, covenantal ethics requires an element of the gratuitous. A potential conflict, however, emerges between the two characteristics of responsiveness and gratuitous service. Response to debt and gratuitous service seem to be opposed principles of action.

This conflict results when one abstracts the concept of covenant from its original context in the transcendent. One cannot fully appreciate the indebtedness of a human being by toting up the varying sacrifices and investments made by others in his or her favor. The sense that one inexhaustibly receives presupposes a more transcendent source of donative activity than the sum of gifts received from others. In the biblical tradition this transcendent source secretly gives root to every gift between human beings, a source that the human order of giving and receiving can only (and imperfectly) signify. Jewish farmers obedient to the injunction to leave something for the sojourner did not simply respond mathematically to earlier gifts received from Egyptians or from strangers drifting through their own land. At the same time, they did not act gratuitously. Their ethic of service to the needy flowed from Israel's original and continuing state of neediness and indebtedness before God. Thus action that at a human level appears gratuitous, in that a specific gratuity from another human being does not provoke it, still, at its deepest level, as gift, answers to gift. The New Testament expresses this responsivity theologically as follows: "In this is love, not that we loved God but that he loved us. . . . If God so loved us, we also ought to love one another" (1 John 4:10–11). In some such way, covenantal ethics, grounded in the transcendent, shies away from the idealist assumption of wholly gratuitous professional action and also from the contractualist assumption that quotidian self-interest should govern every exchange.

A transcendent reference may also help lay out not only the larger horizon in which human service takes place but also the specific standards by which we should measure it. Earlier we noted some dangers in reducing rights and duties to the terms of a particular contract. We observed the need for a transcendent norm that measures and limits contracts. By the same token, rights and duties should not wholly derive from the particulars of a given covenant. What limits ought to be placed on the demands of an excessively dependent patient? At what point does the keeping of one covenant do an injustice to obligations entailed in others? These questions warn against a conventional ethic that sentimentalizes any and all involvements, without reference to a transcendent that both justifies and measures them.

## Covenantal Ethics Applied

If a covenantal ethic is responsive, what goal or goals define the content of that response? What human good does (or should) the medical profession pursue? Our discussions on the shaman, the parent, and the fighter cumulatively suggest that neither resistance, avoidance, nor the quietistic acceptance of suffering and death should define the healer's task, but rather pursuit of health and, let it be noted, the extension of a healing care in the midst of disintegrating health. An ancient and positive etymological link exists between "holy," "healing," and "making whole"; between "salve" and "salvation." Leon Kass emphasizes health as the determinative goal of medicine, which he defines in its classical sense as the well-working of an organism as a whole.[20] To promote this "well-working" is the healer's fundamental goal. It emphasizes preventive and rehabilitative care as well as crisis intervention. Edmund Pellegrino rightly contends that health cannot be the exclusive goal of practice without undercutting the physician's responsibility for care in the midst of the patient's failing health. The organism may never work well again as a whole, but the physician still must "heal" in the sense of helping to keep the distracted patient whole in the face of ineliminable adversity. Either way, the tasks of the healer define themselves positively.

Needless to say, this more positive vision of the healer's role does not altogether eliminate a military component in the healing process. The fight against suffering and death has an important and contributory, but subordinate, relation to the positive goal of health. The biblical position does not imply that the three responses to death of flight, fight, and acceptance have no validity whatsoever. Although the avoidance of death becomes unwholesome when it assumes the proportions of frantic denial, the prudent avoidance of harm and injury is an obligation for those who take seriously a creative and nurturant God. Although a resistance to death takes a grim toll on patients and families alike when it escalates into unconditional warfare, the fight against death has a subordinate, but positive, place in a faith that would respect and conserve life. Although Christians and Jews should not worship death ("You shall have no other gods before me"), they should prepare for it fittingly. The anticipation of death need not mean worship of it; and such anticipation and preparation, with God's grace, may help to make the avoidance of death a little less desperate and the fight against it a little less grim. Released from a metaphysically desperate sense of the human condition, the professional may pursue a little more freely the primary goal of health care.

Questions still remain about the quality control and tenor of that care. This chapter closes, therefore, with a discussion of the implications of a covenantal ethic for relationships to colleagues (the issue of professional self-regulation) and to patients (the virtue of fidelity).

*1. Professional Self-Regulation and Discipline.* The problem of lax professional self-regulation and discipline dates to the Hippocratic tradition, with which this chapter began. The ancient oath distinguished between codal duties to patients and covenantal obligations to the physician's teacher and his progeny. The latter acquire a gravity that gives them precedence over obligations to patients, because they flow from the student's indebtedness to the teacher. When concern for the teacher (or, by extension in the modern world, professional colleagues) dominates, professional ethics reduces itself to courtesy within a guild. Responsibilities to patients (such as informing them about incompetent treatment) do not simply disappear; professionals deny them; professionals view such reports as a breach of the discretionary bonds that pertain in the guild. Thus an inversion occurs. A report on incompetent or unethical behavior to patients becomes a breach in "professional ethics," that is, a breach in courtesy.

For many reasons, social, religious, and cultural, doctors in the modern world duck responsibility for professional self-criticism and regulation. First, like any professional group, doctors find themselves in a complex, interlocking network of relationships with fellow professionals: They extend favors; incur debts; exchange referrals; intertwine personal histories. The bond with fellow professionals grows, while ties with patients seem transient. Furthermore, an organization directed to specific ends tends to generate a sense of community among professional staff members serving those ends. The experience of collegiality can become an end in its own right and subtly take precedence over the needs of the population served. Hence, professional life inevitably mutes criticism.

Second, doctors, more than other professionals, may find self-regulation more difficult to achieve because public criticism seems somewhat more natural to lawyers and academicians, whose work goes on in an adversarial or at least a disputatious setting. The doctor, however, plays a special role in relation to his or her patients, the quasi-priestly-parental; public criticism would seem to subvert this role. Even if one breaks free of the parental-priestly model, trust remains an important ingredient in the relationship; free-ranging criticism erodes trust.

Third, the physician's authority, while great, is precarious. The analogy often drawn between the authority of the modern doctor and the traditional power of parent and priest obscures an important difference between them in the security of their status. The modern doctor walks a high wire. Many patients apotheosize the doctor, but they bitterly resent him if his hand slips publicly but once.

The reason for this precariousness of status lies in differing sources of authority. Parents and priests in traditional society derive their authority from sacred powers perceived as largely creative, nurturant, and beneficent. Given this derivation from positive power, laypeople could tolerate some human defect in the religious authority figure. The power of good would prevail despite human lapse. The modern doctor's authority, however, derives reflexively from a grim negativity, that is, from the fear of death. The same power of death that exalts physicians and makes them the most highly paid and authoritative professionals in the modern world threatens to bring them low if through their own negligence, unscrupulousness, or incompetence they endanger the life of a patient. Thus although modern physicians enjoy much more prestige and authority than contemporary teachers or lawyers, they risk a nasty fall. Resentment against them can flare out. Professional self-criticism in academic life or in the law seems like child's play compared with medicine. The mediocre teacher deprives me merely of the truth; the negligent lawyer forfeits my money or, at worst, my freedom; but the incompetent doctor endangers my life. The stakes seem much higher in the case of medicine. The profession draws its wagons into a circle to protect its members when challenged.

Fourth, Americans in all walks of life have a morally healthy suspicion of officiousness. They press charges against their neighbors or colleagues only reluctantly. They do not like the hypocrisy of those zealous about the sliver in their neighbor's eye while unmindful of the beam in their own. One ought to tend to one's own professional conduct, but beyond that, live and let live. After all, who can tell the difference between an honest mistake and culpable negligence? Who can know enough about a particular medical case to second-guess the physician in charge? Better to keep one's mouth shut. Must a physician be his or her colleague's keeper?

This revulsion against officiousness deserves sympathy, but it fails to respect fully the special covenantal obligations of the professional. Professionals always claim the right to pass judgment (in professional matters) on colleagues or would-be colleagues. The society supports this right when it establishes licensing procedures under the control of professionals and backs up these procedures by prosecuting imposters and pretenders. In effect, the state sanctions a monopoly (a limitation on the supply of professionals). To be sure, patients profit from this through higher standards, but the profession also profits—handsomely—financially. If the professional were, in fact, engaged in a freelance competition (as the myth would have it) without the protection of the monopoly, he or she would not fare nearly so well.

Professional accountability, therefore, must extend beyond the question of one's own personal competence to the competence of other guild members. Duty requires professionals to pass judgment on colleagues; otherwise they profit from a monopoly established by the state without enforcing those standards the need for which alone justifies the monopoly. The individual's license to practice derives ultimately from a prior license to license. If the license to practice carries with it the duty to practice well, the license to license carries with it the duty to judge and monitor well. In professional ethics today, the test of moral seriousness may depend not simply on personal compliance with moral principles but on the courage to hold others accountable. Otherwise the doctor's responsibility to patients yields to the somewhat tarnished privilege of the guild.

The effort to deepen a sense of responsibility for professional self-regulation by appeal to covenantal responsibilities to the profession, to patients, and to the society at large should not lead to the exclusion of some of those values best symbolized by code and contract. Those who live by a code of technical proficiency have a standard on the basis of which to discipline their peers. As noted earlier, Hemingway's novels emphasize discipline. Those who live by a code know how to ostracize deficient peers. Medicine, no exception, relies chiefly on the power of the referral system to isolate the incompetent colleague and contain that person's power to harm.

Defenders of an ethic based on code might argue further that deficiencies in enforcement today result largely from a too strongly developed sense of covenantal obligations to colleagues than from a too weakly developed sense of code. From this perspective, a covenantal ethic creates a problem for professional discipline rather than providing the basis for its amendment. Covenantal obligations to colleagues inhibit the enforcement of duties to patients.

A code alone, however, does not in and of itself solve the problem of professional discipline. It provides only a basis for excluding from one's own inner circle an incompetent physician. But, as Eliot Freidson has pointed out in *Professional Dominance*, the incompetent professional today, when excluded from a given hospital, group practice, or circle of referring colleagues, simply moves his or her practice and finds another circle of equally incompetent colleagues with whom it is possible to function.[21] Given a mobile society with a scarcity of doctors—at least in some areas—the device of local ostracism simply passes on problem physicians to other patients elsewhere. It does not address them. It would take a much more active comprehensive sense of covenantal obligation to all patients on the part of the profession to enforce standards in the guild beyond the locally limited and informal patterns of ostracism.

Codal patterns of discipline, moreover, not only fall short of adequate protection for the patient; they also fail in collegial responsibility to the troubled physician. Those who ostracize handle a colleague lazily when they fail altogether to make a first attempt at remedy and to address the physician personally in his or her difficulty.

At the same time, the indispensable interest and pride of the medical profession in technical proficiency should not lapse because of an expressed preference for a professional ethics based on covenant. Covenantal fidelity to the patient remains unrealized if it does not include proficiency. A rather sentimental existentialism unfortunately assumes that it morally suffices for human beings to be "present" to one another. But in crisis, the ill person needs not simply presence but skill, not just personal concern but highly disciplined services targeted to specific needs. Covenantal ethics, then, must include rather than exclude the interests of the unwritten codes of the profession in the refinement of technical skills.

Neither should a preference for a covenantal ethic lead to the exclusion of the interests of an enforceable contract. Although the reduction of medical ethics to a contract alone incurs the danger of minimalism, patients should have recourse against those physicians who fail to meet minimal standards. They should not depend entirely on disciplinary measures undertaken in the profession. They should retain the right to appeal to the law in cases of malpractice or breaches of contract, explicit or implied.

On the other hand, a legal appeal cannot correct an injustice without assistance and testimony from physicians who take their obligations to patients and their profession seriously. If, in such cases, fellow physicians simply mill around and protect their colleague like a wounded elephant, the patient with just cause probably will not secure redress in the courts. Thus the instrument of contract and other avenues of legal redress rely on physicians who have a deep sense of obligation to the patient and the profession. Needless to say, professional discipline and continuing education vigorously pursued within the profession could cut down drastically on the number of cases that need to reach the courts. But this takes a depth of commitment to the profession and the patients that exceeds minimalist demands under the law. In brief, covenantal fidelity includes the codal duty to become technically proficient; it includes the obligation to meet the minimal terms of contract, but it also requires much more. This more intense obligation, moreover, may finally help not only patients but also troubled colleagues.

*2. Fidelity to the Patient.* The foregoing contrast between a contract and a covenant points toward fidelity as the defining professional virtue. The physician and other health care practitioners owe a double fidelity, both to a body of knowledge that aids and abets healing and to the patient who benefits from the healer's art. Physicians receive pay for their work. The professional exchange partly conforms to a marketplace exchange of buying and selling. But the professional exchange also transcends, or ought to transcend, the cash nexus; it must be disinterested rather than self-interested, and, where necessary, transformational rather than merely transactional.

Buyers and sellers in the marketplace meet as two frankly self-interested and relatively knowledgeable parties. Both sides are justifiably wary. However, patients cannot obey the marketplace warning, "Buyer beware." Their very limited medical knowledge and often confused perception of self-interest hardly protect them. An asymmetry exists between the professional's knowledge and therefore power and the patient's relative ignorance and powerlessness. This imbalance requires that the professional exchange take place in a fiduciary setting of trust that transcends the marketplace assumptions about two wary bargainers. Only the physician's fidelity to the patient in the disposition of his or her knowledge and power justifies that trust. Fidelity requires disinterested discernment, judgment, and action on behalf of the patient's best interest and well-being.

The temptation to depart from disinterested fidelity to the patient takes two forms: overtreatment and undertreatment. The fee-for-service system generally tempts the practitioner to overtreat the patient, especially with acute-care interventions. Fee for service, a contracted piecework payment system, says, in effect, the more discrete pieces of work, the more compensation. Hospitals and doctors alike tend to dice up work into distinct, identifiable procedures, each qualifying for compensation, the cumulative effect of which is to overtreat patients with acute-care services, precisely those services that the system can identify as separate, objective procedures. In a sense, the fee-for-service system also tempts the practitioner to undertreat or mistreat by failing to compensate adequately for those sometimes more thoughtful, sometimes less dramatic, modes of care that the ill and the dying may need. Recent adjustments in the federal fee schedules, which now pay less to the doers and more to the thinkers in medicine (less to surgeons, radiologists, and anesthesiologists, more to internists and deliverers of primary care), increase the rewards for the reflective work patients need. The fee-for-service system also fails to compensate sufficiently those many unglamorous caregivers who provide services for patients in their homes or in nursing homes where care for the chronically ill and the dying might more humanely take place. Disinterested professional service should not mean undercompensated professional service.

The current trends in the third-party payment system have moved the United States increasingly in the direction of undertreatment. The burgeoning growth of for-profit health maintenance organizations (HMOs) and preferred provider organizations (PPOs), which often contract to compensate physicians with bonuses based on the difference between a standard capitation payment per patient and the cost of health services delivered, tends to encourage timely preventative medicine. Early treatment generally tends to reduce the costs of care. But the profit incentives that some HMOs and PPOs tie to reduced costs can tempt practitioners, hospitals, and delivery organizations to undertreat patients and thus compromise fidelity to the patient. This temptation affects not simply the delivery of acute care but also some of those services that might reduce the suffering of the elderly, the dying, and their families. For example, some HMOs and PPOs deny payment for adequate mental health services. (This omission led the American Psychiatric Association to state at its annual meeting in 1994 that the psychiatrist has an ethical obligation to tell the patient [or family in the case of the marginally competent] that a treatment is indicated, whether or not the HMO or PPO will approve of the care. But the HMO or PPO can often drop without cause the psychiatrist who has presented the organization with this awkwardness! Systemic pressures of this sort can make it difficult to practice the virtue of disinterested fidelity to the patient: A system that imposes martyrdom on ordinary virtue is, to say the least, somewhat faulty.)

The covenantal professional exchange differs in a second way from a contractual, marketplace transaction. In addition to its disinterestedness, it is, for want of a better word, transformational, not merely transactional. The healer must respond not simply to the patient's self-perceived wants but to his or her deeper needs. The patient suffering from insomnia often wants simply the quick fix of a pill. But if the physician goes after the root of the problem, then he or she may have to help the patient transform the habits that led to the symptom of sleeplessness. The physician is slothful if he or she dutifully offers acute care but neglects to look for the beginning of an illness and offer preventive medicine. Rehabilitative medicine, and long-term and terminal care also engage the healer in the task of transforming patients. The victim of a heart attack, cancer, or a stroke suffers major changes in body and circumstance, which reflexively call for changes in habits and skills in the course of rehabilitative and long-term care.

As covenantal fidelity requires and inspires healers to engage in responding to patients' deeper needs, the conventional quandary of truth-telling in medicine takes on a different look. Moralists usually reduce the quandary of telling the truth to the question of whether to tell the truth. Consequentialists seek to answer the question by calculating the goods and harms produced by the truth, evasion, or lying. They prize the virtue of benevolence. Duty-oriented moralists tend to argue for the truth irrespective of consequences. A lie wrongs the patient even when it does no harm. Managing the patient, even for benevolent reasons, subverts the patient's dignity. Only the truth respects the patient as a rational creature. Such moralists thus prize foremost the virtue of honesty.

The virtue of covenantal fidelity expands the question of truth-telling in the moral life. Truth becomes a question not only of telling the truth but of being-true. This assertion rests on more than a play on words. The foundational truth of God in Scripture is that God is faithful to his promises. His covenant faithfulness grounds and sustains the world, makes possible our knowledgeable access to it and our performance in it. The very possibility of making truthful assertions rests ultimately on a being-true, a steadfastness that creates and sustains the world. Fidelity on the human scene in all its imperfection reflects in a small way this more spacious ontological setting.

J. I. Austin once drew the distinction, now famous, between two kinds of utterances: descriptive and performative. In ordinary descriptive sentences, one points to or characterizes a given item in the world. (It is raining. The tumor is malignant.) In performative utterances, however, one alters the world by introducing an ingredient that would not be there apart from the utterance. Promises make such performative declarations. (I, John, take thee, Mary. We will defend your country in case of attack. I will not abandon you.) To make a promise alters the world of the person to whom one extends the promise. Conversely, defecting from a promise can be world shattering.

Medical ethics treats the question of truth-telling entirely at the level of descriptive speech. Should the doctor tell the patient that he or she has a malignancy? If not, may one lie, or must one merely withhold the truth?

The notion of performative speech expands the question of truth-telling in professional life. Physicians and nurses face the moral question not simply of telling the truth, but of being true to their word. Conversely, the total situation for a patient includes not only the disease one has but also whether others desert or stand by a person in this extremity. The fidelity of others does not eliminate the disease, but it mightily affects the human context in which the disease runs its course. The doctor offers a patient not simply proficiency and diagnostic accuracy but also fidelity.

Thus the virtue of fidelity begins to affect the resolution of the dilemma itself. Perhaps more patients and clients could accept the descriptive truth if they experienced the performative truth. The anxieties of patients in terminal illness compound because they fear that professionals will abandon them. Perhaps patients would be more inclined to trust the doctor's performative utterances if they trusted diagnoses and prognoses. That is why a cautiously wise medieval physician once advised his colleagues: "Promise only fidelity!"

Furthermore, truth-telling raises not merely the substantive question as to *whether* one tells the truth, but *how* one tells it directly or indirectly, personally or with a sparing impersonality. As the saying goes, "It is not only what you say, but when and how you say it." The theologian Karl Barth once observed that Job's friends were metaphysically correct in what they had to say, but existentially false in their timing, and therefore ultimately false theologically. They chose a miserable moment to sing their theological arias on the subject of suffering.

Prudence in these matters demands much more than shrewdness in knowing how to package what one has to say. Discretion depends on metaphysical perception, a sense for what the Stoics called the fitting, a discretion that discerns more deeply than mere tact, a feel for behavior congruent with reality. Death may not be ultimate, but its sting nevertheless hurts. One must respect that fact. Without *discretion* professionals do not reckon with the whole truth. They may tell the truth, but they do not serve the truth when they tell it. They may use the truth to serve their own vanity; or to satisfy their own craving for power over their patients; or to indulge themselves in the role of nag, policeman, pedant, or judge.

The physician finds telling the truth easier in those cases where the patient and physician can do something together to prevent a disease or cure it, but it also matters as a part of healing in terminal illness. Healing "makes whole." The physician and the patient may not be able to knock out the cancer that kills. But they may still go a long way toward keeping the patient whole or intact even in extremity. This is part of the hard opportunity in truth-telling. But it depends on much more than the readiness of the physician to dispense sentence pellets of the truth about the patient's condition. Such pellets, unsupported by faithful care and by care that takes the form of sensitive teaching, can be lethal and anything but respectful of patients. Thus the question of the truth expands beyond decision bits and raises the question of the healer's readiness to accept his or her role as teacher in the therapeutic enterprise.

What does it mean to be a health care professional?

what are your obligation + responsibilities?

To whom do your obligations + responsibilities extend?

What is the Nature of your obligations + responsibilities?

GIFT → COVENANT

## Chapter Five

# Teacher

The covenantal image, alone among the major images treated in this book, demands that healers teach their patients. Other images—those of parent, technician, fighter, and contractor—may do so incidentally, but at best they usually generate ambivalence toward the teaching function.

The parental image tends to reduce patients to dependent children, stricken sheep. Compassionate care and vicarious decision making rather than candid instruction characterize the professional's task. Only too often, parentalist healers, like Dostoevsky's Grand Inquisitor, have a low estimate of their charges and want to protect them from that turmoil that knowledge and freedom entail.

The location of many teaching hospitals and residency training programs in the inner city tends further to convince young professionals that preventive medicine and the teaching it requires are activities of low yield. Residents complain that patients often come in only when their diseases flare. Preventive medicine seems beside the point. Destructive habits so grip the patient as to make rehabilitation or stable chronic care difficult to sustain. After treatment, patients go back into the streets and fall into the same injurious habits again. They forget appointments; they do not comply with a regimen. Patients say: "I don't know what medicines I take. It's in the chart. Read the chart." But the resident knows that the chart records what the physician prescribed, not what the patient is taking, if anything.

Furthermore, patients fear the truth or fail to assimilate it or accept it but selectively. Some pounce on the bad news and panic; others dissolve the bad news in a blurry confusion and ignore the importance of compliance. In response, physicians retreat into a limited parentalist mode, making decisions on behalf of the patient in the sanctuary of the hospital, knowing that the world beyond the hospital walls will shortly defeat their childlike charges. Thus, early in their education physicians come to expect very little from patients. Cynicism, despair, and sometimes resentment infect the exhausted resident.

And yet—even parentalism offers some moral warrant for teaching one's patients. The parent, after all, is committed to the being and well-being of the child, and the good parent recognizes education as an important ingredient in the child's flourishing. The main thrust of the image, however, condescends too much to encourage persistent teaching. Give what care you can to hurting charges and let it go at that.

To the degree that practitioners think of themselves only as contractors dispensing technical services they also tend to depreciate the place of teaching in therapy. Contracted for and paid on a piecework basis, whether by the consumer personally or by a third-party payment system, the therapist offers discrete, itemizable services rather than taking continuous responsibility for the patient's improvement in self-care and health maintenance. Teaching takes time; it reduces the number of patients the physician can see; it complicates the question of patient management and exposes the physician to the possibility of making personal as well as technical errors. Both the specialist and the generalist can draw back from teaching the patient—the specialist offering encoded information to the attending physician, and the attending physician sometimes reneging on the task by defining himself or herself chiefly as the orchestrator of technical services. And yet the contractualist model retains a fragment of the teaching responsibility, to the degree that the seller of services accepts responsibility to inform the buyer about the services and the product offered for sale. Furthermore, health maintenance organizations (HMOs) draw up contracts with their patients that give professionals financial incentives to teach better.

The military model hardly emphasizes the physician as teacher. It conjoins the technical and contractual models with an adversarial setting to produce the mercenary who fights against disease and death. The patient has fallen victim to invasive powers. Amateurs mucking about with weapons that they hardly understand will only blow themselves up. A little knowledge is a dangerous thing. The expert in biological warfare should decide which drugs best counter the intricacies of the enemy's attack, its time, its place, and its force. Besides, under the conditions of battle, with the physician fighting on behalf of a thousand little principalities, explaining wastes time.

Both the economics of medicine and the structure of medical education reinforce the tendency of physicians, who live by the technical-contractualist-military models, to neglect teaching. The third-party payment system rewards physicians for discrete, piecework services to the sick. It does not reward them for teaching patients how to maintain their health or even for securing high levels of compliance with the doctor's regimen. Not surprisingly, a President's Committee on Health Care Education reported for 1973 that only one-half of 1 percent of annual health care expenditures went for health education.[1] Although HMOs make a good-faith effort to redirect the economic incentives toward preventive medicine, the high turnover rates of patient subscribers in HMOs (30 percent per year) do not suggest that those organizations have succeeded in giving the professional much financial incentive to practice pedagogically persuasive preventive medicine.[2]

Neither medical school education nor residency training programs adequately prepare physicians for teaching. Professional education prepares them as depositories of information, not sharers of what they know. "Medicine is the only graduate school to rely on multiple choice examinations," complains one academic physician.[3] Sadly enough, this subarticulate standard of testing fails to challenge the student to organize and teach effectively, or even to retain what he or she knows. According to a study of a second-year class at a distinguished medical school, the half-life of a retained factual item is about three weeks; 90 percent of factual items retained for true-false examinations have taken flight by graduation.[4]

Cumulatively, a professional education that centers on the mere acquisition of factual information converts education itself from a public trust to privately held property. The student soon assumes that he or she has acquired knowledge as a private stockpile of goods to be sold wholly as the certified possessor sees fit. The information that lab tests, X rays, and biopsies yield belongs to the professional rather than to the patient whose destiny they foretell. And patients often submit to this view. They would feel as shy about reading the physician's workup of their case—while he or she is out of the office—as about reading any other papers or letters on the desk. Such information seems like private property, for the physician alone to divulge. Thus the very terms of professional education and clinical training and practice combine to obscure the communal origins of professional education and the duty to share generously what one knows.

The quarrel in medicine over whether physicians should teach their patients is not new; it dates back to the classical world. The "rough empirics" in ancient Greece (who, familiar with treatments but not with the scientific reasons for their success, practiced largely on slaves) used to ridicule the more scientifically oriented physicians (who, practicing largely on free men and their families, sought to teach their patients). The scientific physicians complained that the empirics offered little more than what Lain Entraigo has called a veterinary practice on humans. But the empirics argued that patients do not want to become doctors; they want to be cured.

Modern technicians have argued a fortiori that the knowledge base of medicine has grown so complicated as to make the effort to teach patients today even more futile than in ancient Greece. Physicians do not share a common scientific understanding with even their most educated patients. The knowledge explosion has produced in our time a fallout of ignorance. And because knowledge confers power, the ignorant, to the extent of their ignorance, become powerless. For better or for worse, patients can only submit themselves to the superior knowledge, authority, good intentions, and technical ingenuity of the doctor.

And yet, modern technology itself has allowed us in many respects to break with the understanding of disease that heretofore has minimized the teaching role of the healer. Traditionally interpreted, disease seemed to erupt episodically, breaking health and suspending the normal discretion that the patient exercises over his or her life. On falling ill, one surrenders one's natural authority until, through the mysterious interventions of the physician, a return to the normal world becomes possible. As the analogy has it, disease disrupts health the way war interrupts peace. This irruptive and episodic account of disease, however, overlooks what Horacio Fabrega of Michigan State University has called the processive character of both disease and health.[5] Long before symptoms appear, the cardiovascular system may be preparing for catastrophe. A processive understanding of disease (which sophisticated monitoring devices make accessible to the modern practitioner) argues for a more collaborative interpretation of the physician-patient relationship. The physician must function as teacher, sharing information with the patient and engaging the layperson more actively to maintain good health. The professional charged with care needs to serve as more than a technician; for technology itself provides the physician with early warning of diseases that may respond to professionally assisted self-care.

The covenantal image for the health care practitioner pushes the profession unequivocally in the direction of teaching. To the degree that physicians and institutions accept a covenantal responsibility for the being and well-being of their patients—above and beyond the delivery of technical services—they must engage in the delicate business of transforming their patients' habits. The prevention of disease, the recovery from a siege of illness, and the successful coping with chronic conditions require, in one form or another, the reconstruction of lifestyles. Whenever healers engage in these activities, they transform rather than merely transact. They do not simply offer services to satisfy the wants and wishes of people as they are; they engage in transforming commitments, priorities, and life rhythms.

But any professional effort to transform patients flirts with danger. It can quickly deteriorate into a puritanical officiousness—a runaway parentalism—unless teaching becomes its chief instrument. Teaching offers one of the few ways in which one can engage in transformation while respecting the patient's intelligence and power of self-determination. Good teaching depends not only on a direct grasp of one's subject, a desire to share it, and some verbal facility; it also requires a kind of moral imagination that permits one to enter into the life circumstances of the learner: to reckon with the difficulties the learner faces in acquiring, assimilating, and acting on what he or she needs to know. Good teachers do not attempt to transform their students by bending them against their will, or by charming them out of their faculties, or by managing them behind their backs. Rather, they help them see their lives and their habits in a new light and thereby aid them in unlocking a freedom to perform in new ways.

Teaching has a place in medical practice across a broad spectrum of activities. Obviously, preventive, rehabilitative, chronic, and terminal care includes a teaching component. Because the educational task of the physician shows least obviously in those activities in which physicians intervene most, this brief tour of the horizon ought to begin with the physician's efforts to cure.

## Acute Care Medicine

Except for the most aggressive of interventions, therapy requires some measure of cooperation from the patient. But noncompliance rates range from 30 to 60 percent of patients, and even higher in those cases in which patients suffer no painful symptoms.[6] Those percentages are extraordinarily high. A clinical drug test would probably disappoint if it failed to help 30 to 60 percent of patients treated. No obstacle looms quite so large as noncompliance in impeding effective intervention.

Strategies for enhancing compliance depend on improving the physician's prowess as a teacher. One study shows that rates of compliance doubled from 29 to 54 percent depending on whether instructors provided low or high levels of instruction.[7] "Words are to a prescription what a preamble is to a constitution," as Lain Entralgo, the Spanish historian of medicine, once argued. The Preamble to the Constitution of the United States ("We, the People of the United States, in Order to form a more perfect Union . . .") provides a clarifying context that makes sense and provides purpose for the laws that follow. Without that preamble, the fundamental law of the land just sits there, opaque, arbitrary, and perhaps relatively unintelligible to subsequent generations. Even God provided a context for his commands. Before issuing the Ten Commandments, Scripture reports, God announced and explained to the Israelites the grounds for their obedience:

> I am the LORD your God, who brought you out
> of the land of Egypt, out of the house of
> bondage. (Ex. 20:2)

The reminder about these deeds explains the commandments that follow: "You shall have no other gods before me. You shall not . . ." When physicians issue prescriptions wordlessly, opaquely, without an earnest effort to clarify and persuade, they do not play God; they usurp another kind of privilege, high-handed, arrogant, and ultimately obtuse. One thinks of Kierkegaard's characterization of the demonic state in *The Concept of Dread.*[8] He describes it as "shut-upness," a dreadful taciturnity, unrevealing, unhelpful, withdrawn, and cruelly destructive to those who need a healing word.

Every profession depends on an esoteric body of knowledge, encoded by specialists and relatively inaccessible to the layperson. What has been carefully encoded needs decoding, and that process requires adept teaching. Not surprisingly, then, the literature on compliance emphasizes those strategies prized by the good teacher. Physicians must teach early in the game (one of the most stubborn obstacles to compliance springs from the patient's conviction that the original diagnosis itself is wrong);[9] they must teach clearly in nontechnical language (decoding); they produce better results when they offer the explanation in both oral and written form; and whatever they say, they must organize well. They have to allow for a period in the course of which the patient internalizes the news. Doctors partly condemn the learning capacity of their patients because they fail to appreciate the patient's need for repetition and for time to assimilate the diagnostic and prognostic news, which is sometimes difficult to bear.

Information simply unloaded on the patient sits like a parallel deposit in the mind, unassimilated and inert.

Compliance rates also improve when the physician teaches not only the patient but the patient's family. Efforts at weight loss, control of hypertension and arthritis, and recovery programs after heart attacks show better results when the family actively supports the program.[10] Problems of compliance in these areas raise questions about the place of teaching in preventive and rehabilitative medicine.

## Preventive Medicine

Physicians and the public at large, until recently, have held preventive medicine in low esteem. Hygeia, the goddess of health, has never been a match for the god of healing. Asclepius always appears in full feather, the quintessentially male, TV-spectacular agent of interventionist medicine. Since the discovery of penicillin and the antibiotics, money for research and health delivery has gone largely to acute care. Expenditures in the name of Asclepius rose 800 percent in the two decades following World War II.[11] The third-party payment system, under public and private insurance programs, has tilted in almost every detail toward curative medicine. The fraction of funds going into health education has remained constant and minuscule (about one-half of 1 percent) whereas the portion of the GNP devoted to health care has risen astronomically during the period 1940–1981.[12] Yet, during this same period—except for the success of antibiotics, mind-control drugs, and some surgical procedures—the actual advances in acute care have not been all that striking. The life expectancy of fifty-year-old white males during two decades rose only eight months despite the most generous expenditure of funds and talent on acute care in world history.[13]

The goddess Hygeia symbolizes the condition of health rather than the activity of healing: the steadfast rule of reason in body care rather than the rule of ingenuity in body repair; the balanced classical concern for dietetics and gymnastics rather than the more occult appeals to special nostrums, insights, and powers. But, alas, Hygeia has always been, and ever will be, a dull gray goddess, without box-office draw or fundraising appeal. W. Hutchinson saw the structural problem with a steady eye when he wrote:

> The system of remuneration makes the physician's income dependent upon the amount of sickness. Our system's philosophy might be condensed in the motto "millions for the care and not one cent for prevention." It seems to me that the weakness of our system lies in this one fact, that it gives [physicians] such exceedingly little opportunity for what has been called the practice of preventive medicine.[14]

Hutchinson wrote these lines in 1886.

The obstacles to the development of preventive medicine do not come entirely from physicians— either from their economic self-interest or from a special perception of role that discourages good teaching. Four types of patients, even under the best of circumstances, make the task of preventive medicine a slow boring through hard wood (Max Weber's phrase about another difficult vocation—politics). Patients of the first type assume their own de facto immortality. Someday they will die, but not yet. Disease and death for the moment remain abstract, deferrable, and remote. They feel the medicine of immortality already within them. They do not need preventive medicine. Patients of the second type seem less given to denial. They go to the doctor and listen to all the explanations. But the doctor discovers on the next visit that none of it sinks in. A kind of selective interferon seems at work, blocking out what the doctor has to say. The patient has internalized nothing.

At the opposite extreme are those patients given to what Robert Jay Lifton, in another connection, called nuclearism. Such persons solve the problem of threat by cozying up to the source of danger. Contact with the forbidden, the destructive, magnifies their life. The actor Slim Pickens, in the film *Dr. Strangelove*, portrays a country colonel who straddles a nuclear bomb and ecstatically rides it to his own destruction. Nuclearists feel drawn to the pull of the cigarette, the regular swell of liquor in the head, the helmetless ride on a motorcycle at high speed, the pressure cooker of a job, the brinkmanship with the psyche that goes with drugs and sleep deprivation. Recklessness in all its forms acquires a kind of demonic force that makes all the cautionary advice and counsel of preventive medicine seem beside the point and demeaning.

Finally, there are the hypochondriacs. Like the nuclearists, they preoccupy themselves with danger, but in this case they let danger provide them with an excuse for diminishing their life. Hypochondriacs see trouble on every side, risk at every corner, poison in the very food they eat, the blast of cancer in the sun, a dangerous depletion in every psychic exertion, and the potential for terminal disease in the most transient colony of germs to which they play host. Such persons frustrate preventive medicine. Health alone unhealthily obsesses them, miniaturizes their life, makes them too fearful to exude that health that a life well expended on matters of greater moment sometimes fosters. Encountering patients such as these in their daily experience must dampen physicians' hopes for preventive medicine. So much advice falls on stony ground.

Still, the rate of deaths from heart attack and stroke have declined rapidly in recent years, and the evidence does not suggest that open-heart surgery, resuscitation techniques, and other improved interventions have made the difference in the huge decline. Rather, changes in diet (especially reduced salt intake), regular exercise, reductions in weight, drug compliance for control of hypertension, and other essentially preventive measures seem to account for the improvements in health. This progress hardly results from the teaching efforts of physicians alone. Deeper cultural changes are at work. The magisterial authority of the media and the networking of patient groups play their part in improving self-care. But it would be passing strange for physicians to withdraw from preventive work simply because others as well help to provide it.

The skepticism doctors often betray toward preventive work may result partly from their failure to be imaginative about the social setting in which it should take place. They too readily generalize from their own one-on-one curative work and take for granted the individual tutorial (a little too private to be fully effective) as the only appropriate setting for their teaching. As alternatives to the tutorial in the physician's office, society offers the even more private and isolating spot commercials on television, the bus advertisements, the newspaper columns, or the individual pamphlets distributed by the American Heart Association and American Cancer Society. Physicians largely ignore the fact that most teaching takes place in public classrooms—

from the three Rs to AA. Other, more communal, strategies for educating patients deserve attention.

The chief of clinical services in student health at a large Midwestern university saw just such an opportunity for communal preventive medicine at his campus. Ordinarily, jobs in student health are dull. (Either students seem radiantly healthy and need nothing medical that is more technically complicated than antibiotics and a good night's respite from the dormitory, or they are too sick to remain in school—in which case also the physician does not get to handle an interesting case. Psychiatrists, of course, are an exception in that they get to take care of young students just separated from home whose emotional problems respond best to treatment in situ.) But this young physician—not a psychiatrist—chose a career in student health because he was interested in preventive medicine, and, given that interest, he explained, a university campus offered a splendid opportunity. In its preventive program, his clinic did a health profile of each student on arrival, including a projection of life expectancy on the basis of current habits and a second projection on the basis of an alternative set of habits. Then the clinic, taking advantage of a computer analysis and classification of problems, pulled the potentially hypertensive, the obese, and so on, into a classroom where the health care practitioners taught and worked at their problems collectively.

The program had four advantages over conventional preventive efforts: It picked up patients at a relatively early age; it pulled them into a setting that kept them feeling normal and let them respond normally to their obligations; it provided them with a support group of fellows with a similar problem, thus overcoming the discouraging isolation that young people with special problems feel; and finally, the classroom provided for economies of scale as compared with conventional, expensive tutorial contact with a professional. When a visitor to the campus asked why a similarly motivated health care team could not work with other institutions—such as corporations, unions, service organizations, and churches—the young physician reported that his own group in student health was on the verge of signing a contract with the local Presbyterian church.

A few health care groups have similarly allied themselves with religious communities, but on the whole, the helping professions have not thought through the ways in which they might link with so-called intermediate institutions to offer services directed to prevention and rehabilitation. The dominant model of health care defined by the delivery of services in a freestanding hospital or in a private office has—in addition to its other disadvantages—emphasized the individual at the expense of the communal and the manipulative at the expense of the cognitive in the task of healing.

## Rehabilitative and Chronic Care

In preventive medicine, the physician faces the difficult task of persuading patients that they face real threats to their health. In rehabilitative medicine, few patients can doubt for long the reality of the assault. The patient has just suffered a massive blow to body confidence. An accident maims or disfigures and imposes a catastrophic change on the patient's very self-perception—his or her movement and looks. A coronary suddenly throws the mainspring of life itself into terrible disarray. A stroke slurs speech, renders useless one side of the body, confuses memory and vision, and depresses the spirit. A burn scorches the skin and tightens movement, leaving the victim like a countryside charred and crippled by the firestorm of war; and kidney failure poisons every river in the system, subjecting the victim to impotence and depression.

Patients pass through three stages: (1) Their life brutally changes, and they plunge into shock, numbness, and grief; (2) they suffer a period of perilous transition; until at length (3) they make their way into a new life under the terms and conditions of their disability. The entire process compares structurally with the great rites of passage in traditional societies.

Similarly, the ritual "turning points" in traditional societies—the events associated with puberty, marriage, birth, death, seed time, sickness, and war—included three moments, all of them important to a successful passage. The first moment imposed a radical separation of the participant from his or her past life. Young people undergoing a puberty rite suffered, at the outset, perhaps segregation, whipping, tattooing, or pulling of a tooth. The mutilation visibly signified a death to one's former life. Second, the novitiate underwent a period of transition, with its appropriate regimen and ordeal under the tutelage of specialists. Third, the candidate eventually entered into a new estate. One could not view this new identity as something added onto one's previous life by way of peaceful annexation. A radical alteration had occurred, affecting habits, demands, regimens, and core identity. The relation between old and new resembled a kind of death and resurrection. Calendars reflect this sacral dimension as they order and measure time before and after the event.

Similarly, in the case of personal catastrophe, we measure time before and after—the accident, the heart attack, the stroke, the operation, or the birth of the retarded child.

The role of the modern healer both resembles and differs from that of the religious specialist who presides over traditional rites of passage. First, the healer does not, like the traditional priest, make the first "moment" occur. But he or she has special knowledge of what has taken place and of its convulsive impact on the patient. If the healer served as the attending physician in the case, he or she helped set a limit to its destructive consequences. That special knowledge and service provide a basis for the second role as tutor and guide during the transition period. Or, by referral, the healer helps legitimate those who will take over rehabilitative therapy. Depending on the severity of the accident or the disease, the patient must engage in a drastic reconstruction of habits. One must perhaps learn all over again how to walk, exercise, eat, rest, and pace oneself in daily work.

In addition to helping in the reconstruction of skills, the healer has to reckon with the psychological perils of the transitional period. The sufferer, to be sure, cannot doubt the reality of the problem; the heart attack overwhelms, palpably, beyond compare, but all outsize events, whether good or bad, have their own unreality. "Has this really happened to me? It hardly seems possible. It won't be there when I wake up in the morning." Alternatively, the patient descends into despair—another kind of unreality that obscures the resources of both therapy and the gathering inner resources that the passage of time places at the patient's own disposal. Or again, the patient passes beyond the confusion and disorientation of the original assault into the ordered procedures of the institution that has provided treatment, but this alien order still seems unreal because so patently not his or her own.

When the patient begins tentatively, almost experimentally, to take hold of the rehabilitating regimen, then that person may move suddenly out of numbness, despair, and confusion and be inclined to overestimate touchingly and pathetically the speed of recovery—expecting rapid strides back into the old familiar world—only to experience a setback, physical and psychological, that signals a far more protracted period of recovery. And then, still later, there is the discovery that one recovers not only slowly but incompletely. The patient will never become again the person he or she once was, "as good as new," but a different human being, permanently limited in one way or another, and inwardly altered by this ordeal.

And yet a third stage eventually comes when the patient reenters the world, a world itself not quite the same, shadowed in some ways, poignantly heightened in others, as skills once taken for granted now seem almost miraculous, and as sounds and smells hitherto unnoticed seem a grace note in life. Friendships and family bonds stretch and rearrange—in some cases deepen, in others tragically weaken—until at length one's powerful link with the attending physician, physical therapist, or occupational therapist, one's mentor and guide, as it were, ends.

The company of those who serve as tutors to patients may include not only the attending physician and nurse but also physical therapists, occupational therapists, workers on various outpatient services, and, last but hardly least, other patients who have themselves survived a similar ordeal.

Most healers other than the physician, both by training and conviction, acknowledge the importance of teaching. In fact, the best teaching I witnessed during a year as an observer at a hospital came from a family health care practitioner who worked under the auspices of an inner-city clinic with links to the teaching hospital. This paraprofessional grew up in the ghetto himself and worked under the direction of sophisticated nurses (who warned me before I set out on home visitations with the practitioner that the chief medical problem in the neighborhood was no particular disease but inadequate housing). The family practitioner took me on his rounds to overcrowded, sometimes windowless, vermin-infested apartments, largely occupied by old couples or young mothers and children who either seemed temporarily quelled by visitors or squirmed in the dark. He painstakingly taught his patients and worked just as conscientiously with their family caretakers. The head physician administering the program recognized the social value of this service to the hospital, above and beyond its value to the individual patient. She observed with pride that the hospital-clinic was one of the few buildings in the area spared in the last spate of neighborhood riots. Apparently the institution had kept covenant with the neighborhood. And ghetto residents, even teenagers, respected this fact.

The physician's general neglect of teaching increases the burden on other health care professionals. This substitution sometimes seems an improvement. Training programs in other fields usually emphasize the professional's responsibility to teach not only in rehabilitation but in preventive, curative, and chronic care. But when the physician defaults from teaching and hands on the patient to persons with less clout, the legitimation of authority sometimes suffers. The physician needs to lay the groundwork for what follows even if he or she does not execute in every detail the therapeutic regimen.

Nurses particularly find themselves in a delicate position, in dealing with acute care cases, if they must teach the patient—yet the physician retains full authority over disclosure and neglects the responsibilities that go with that authority. Because the nurse sees the patient constantly while the physician ducks in and out, the emotional strain of failing to level with the patient and the patient's family falls on the nurse's shoulders. Other professionals need the legitimation of authority and direction and technical guidance that the physician can provide, and the physician needs the kind of information that only those who have day-to-day contact with the patient can furnish.

Selected former patients, organized and unorganized, also serve a teaching function. Admittedly, the company of other patients in a similar plight has its risks. They sometimes exhibit a tedious missionary zeal, a paternal officiousness that seeks to dominate through greater experience, half-baked professionalism, or strained cheerfulness. Leaders of support groups usually try to weed out those former patients who have failed to effect successful passage through the illness (sometimes for reasons not at all related to their ordeal). But even those who have reconstructed their life despite catastrophe can depress the newly arrived patient, as they soberly remind that person of the severe handicaps he or she must eventually accept. The pitfalls await, yet the active mentoring performed by former alcoholics, burn victims, heart attack and cancer patients reminds us, in an age that tends to reduce healing to the limited alternatives of professional care or self-care, that instruction often goes on among a company of peers.

## Terminal Care and the Question of Style

The forms of medical care covered so far—curative, preventive, and rehabilitative—demand that the physician teach; terminal care, less obviously so. Teaching seems irrelevant to the ultimate crisis. Indeed, the truth itself appears, at best, out of place; at worst, crushing. In the last chapter, I argued for the truth, but the truth in the context of fidelity. In this context, the truth expands beyond true assertions to the professional's more extended vocation as a teacher. The issue of terminal care now returns us again to the further question of the teacher's style. Clearly, teaching in medical crisis differs from ordinary academic instruction. The teacher deals with a profoundly troubled listener. The news the teacher brings can devastate. One must be wise and tactful in how one tells the truth.

The delicacy of crisis and terminal care forces a further look at the language used in communicating with patients. Our resources in language fall into several categories: (1) direct, immediate, blunt talk; (2) circumlocution or double-talk; (3) silence; and (4) discourse that proceeds—partly, at least—by way of indirection.

Silence, of course, can lead to sharing, but also to evasion. The technical nature of the medical vocabulary provides plenty of opportunities for a second form of evasion—elusive double-talk. Evasion is more difficult to achieve than it appears. Body language and countenance blurt out more than words reveal. Even though physicians manage information, family members cannot do so deftly. The face betrays what the tongue cannot say. So the patient lives with the knowledge, without benefit of whatever additional help the physician might offer. We may deny death but cannot avoid it.

The last decade has seen a huge reaction against the response of silence. Death courses have out-enrolled their competitors in elective offerings at American colleges. Dr. Kübler-Ross achieved celebrity with her book *On Death and Dying*. Broadway has brought forth several plays on the subject. Direct talk on the subject abounds. Too often, however, we assume (especially as Americans) that we can tell the truth only directly, immediately, bluntly. Such talk seems the only alternative to evasive silence or circumlocution. On the subject of sex, for example, we assume that the only alternative to the repressions of the Victorian Age is the tiresome, gabby, explicit discussion of sex imposed on our adolescents from junior high school forward.

However, we can also talk *indirectly* on the weighty subjects of death, religion, and love. Obviously, gabby bluntness in the presence of one dying is wholly inappropriate. It reckons in no way with the solemnity of the event. The physician owes the truth, but not all patients want the truth in exhaustive clinical detail. In such cases, we can surely find some alternatives to blunt talk other than double-talk, a condescending cheerfulness, or a frightening silence.

Perhaps examples of what I mean by indirection will suffice. One doctor reports[15] that many patients brought up the question of their own death in an indirect form: Some asked him, for example, whether he thought they should buy a house, marry, or undergo plastic surgery. The doctor realized that the answer "Yes—surely, go ahead" in a big cheerful voice evaded. On the other hand, the answer "No" stopped discussion. He found it important to tell them that he recognized the importance of the question. From that point on, he could discuss with them their uncertainties, anxieties, and fears. The doctor and the patient could share. The doctor need not dwell on the subject for long; after its acknowledgment, he could proceed to the details of daily life without the change of subject becoming an evasion.

We can achieve indirection in another way. Although it sometimes imposes too much to approach the subject frontally under the immediate pressure of its presence, we can achieve indirection if we discuss death in advance of a crisis. Rabbis, priests, or ministers who suddenly feel tongue-tied and irrelevant in the sickroom get what they deserve if they have not worked through the problem with their people in a series of sermons or in work sessions with lay groups. Words too blunt and inappropriate in the crisis itself may, if spoken earlier, provide an indirect basis for sharing burdens. Physicians may similarly discover that the truth shared earlier provides a basis for weathering subsequent events without having to impose it suddenly in a later crisis.

Professionals should not use the option of indirect language as an excuse for delivering signals so remote as to evade or mislead. At its best, indirect discourse verbally respects rather than avoids reality. A kind of double respect comes into play: a respect both for the solemnity of the event and for the distance that the patient chooses to maintain in his or her relationship to the event. A man who knew that he had cancer once said to his middle-aged son, a writer on the subject of death and dying, "Go easy, Don." The man knew he had cancer. But at the same time, he wanted to establish the distance he wished to maintain between himself, his son, and the imminent event of his death. He did not want his son to favor him with seminar-length discussions on the subject. Only a fool would not have respected this request. Some distancing and indirection occur in our relationship to death.

The language of indirection treats death decorously as a sacred event. Indirection often best suits our approach to the sacred. The Jews did not attempt to look directly on Yahweh's face. They dared not approach God casually and directly. But they also could not avoid God's presence. Jews could hold their ground before their Lord in a relation that was genuine but indirect. So also, we need not dwell directly on the subject of death interminably or avoid it by a condescending cheerfulness wholly inappropriate to the event. Still, two human beings can acknowledge death, if ever so indirectly, and hold their ground before it until parted.

## Medical Education

If physicians must teach their patients well, then it may be necessary to recast premedical and medical education and clinical training. Tucking away the subject of teaching strategies in the Department of Public Health and Community Medicine hardly atones for an education that generally aspires to bestow on its graduates no more articulateness than the hieroglyphs on a prescription bottle.

Until the twentieth century, almost all medical education took place in an apprenticeship system. At the turn of the century, only 10 to 12 percent of physicians had a liberal arts education before entering medical schools. The Flexner report of 1910, however, eventually sited medical education in the university and therefore exposed young premedical students to

the liberal arts.[16] Theoretically, at least, this new institutional location, which required that every candidate
for medical school acquire some background in the
humanities, should have helped produce professionals
more pedagogically skilled than the "rough empirics"
of whom Plato complained. But in fact, an under-
graduate liberal arts education today hardly prepares
students to write or teach well. The liberal arts faculty
at large—not just science teachers—bear responsibility for this failure. Unfortunately, academicians have
assumed that only some of their graduates become
teachers; the rest do not. Therefore, they have treated
teaching as a segregated profession. Nonacademic
professionals merely dispense technical services.
Teaching is, of course, a special profession, but at the
same time a liberal arts education ought to turn out
good teachers whether students go into teaching or
not. Nonacademic professionals must teach, even as
they dispense esoteric services. The lawyer, the states-
man, and the business leader, as well as the physician,
must teach. Accordingly, the teacher in the humanities and the social sciences should learn how to set
requirements for reports, papers, and examinations so
as to produce people who know how to share what
they know (a discipline that at its best also increases
the sharer's own grasp of the subject matter).

Similarly, residency training programs need to
encourage good teaching. In a "teaching hospital"
today, doctors use patients as teaching material;
patients are not themselves taught. The very structure
of morning rounds discourages the teaching of
patients. The attending physician on the floor is
accompanied by a small platoon of young clerks and
residents, all of them bristling with good health. They
stop by a bed under a very considerable time pressure.

Twenty patients must be seen in an hour and fifteen minutes, a ration of but three or four minutes to a bed. The patient, meanwhile, has just awakened. He has spent the night mulling over the five or six things that he wanted to discuss, when suddenly he finds himself confronted by these inspectors, jacked like a deer in the glare of headlights. He has remembered and voiced but one or two things on his list when they move the procession on into the hallway. There the serious teaching takes place as the attending physician and retinue rapidly discuss the case, sotto voce, before traveling to the next room. Young physicians-to-be, of course, surely need the hallway instruction. Patients do serve as teaching material in a teaching hospital. But if residents are to practice competently in their own right, and if teaching is an important part of medical practice, then the teaching hospital should structure education so as to produce professionals who, rather than mutely performing procedures, genuinely profess what they know.

### Teaching among Professional Colleagues

Throughout this chapter, the emphasis has fallen on teaching the patient. Only a fraction of physicians, however, deal with patients. Others function as specialists who abet the work of their colleagues with patients. Such specialists must teach their attending colleagues—discreetly. In the course of delivering technical information, specialists engage in a kind of continuing education. This delicate relationship to colleagues generates opposing moral dangers. Specialists can display, on the one hand, a too-officious, judgmental, and pompous style that condescends toward the generalist and, on the other hand, an obsequiousness that fails in candor, often for the sake of referrals. Particularly specialists at university tertiary-care centers face important moral and political issues of style as they relate to outlying practitioners. A kind of town-gown tension can grow up between the two sets of professionals. The staff at a teaching hospital must teach in such a way as to empower rather than humiliate their colleagues who have responsibility for primary care. Otherwise, the mediocre and defensive practitioner may fail to refer for fear of exposing his or her own inadequacies. This outcome produces not only inconvenient business consequences for the specialist but also more than inconvenient results for future patients who fall into the hands of inadequate caretakers.

Some of the dangers that go with the pomp of hierarchy would abate if the specialist remembered his or her professional debt to the generalist. To be sure, the specialist normally instructs and advises the general practitioner, but often the teaching role is reversed. The specialist needs to learn from, and sometimes to be corrected by, the generalist. The specialist requires, in the first place, the proper flow of information. Furthermore, in case of ambiguous symptoms the specialist sometimes needs to be protected from the tendency to pull a diagnosis in the direction of his or her own particular field of expertise. The generalist alone may possess both the information and the broader perspective crucial to developing the correct differential diagnosis.

The complexity of these interprofessional relationships forces us to close this work with some reflection on a covenantal ethic in an institutional setting. Clearly a covenantal ethic cannot define the internal relationship of a physician to a patient without giving some thought to the physician's task and the institution's responsibility in a socially complex delivery system.

*Chapter Six*

# Covenanted Institutions

A book that traffics in images cannot neglect the question of institutional setting. Increasingly today, professionals nest in large institutions. Physicians are no exception. Medical education itself begins in the great universities; it continues in teaching hospitals; and physicians increasingly work in groups, clinics, and hospital care systems. Not even the solo practitioner escapes the large-scale organization; he or she could not function a single day without the resources provided by institution-based medical research. No more than priests in earlier stages of Western culture have physicians been able to prevent their institutionalization or renounce their dominant place in the hierarchy to which they belong.

Images express and shape the self-perceptions of institutions as well as of individual practitioners. We have already taken marginal note of this fact. The military image shows up in the rigid, hierarchical organization of the hospital and its adversarial thrust against disease. The technical image largely shapes residency training programs and encourages the acquisition of sometimes redundant hardware as hospitals compete with one another for prestige. The teaching image—however neglected in fact—maintains itself institutionally in the very term "teaching hospital." The parental image, unlike the others, seems to have faded today in an institutional setting no longer intimate and familial. Yet the modern hospital has developed impersonal management techniques for handling both patients and their families, which are largely justified on the parentalist ground of the patient's good. Meanwhile, careerists among professionals contractually exploit the moral power of these images and the lax controls of a third-party payment system to amass fortunes. The image of the physician as commercial contractor feeds on the other images, as they seem to offer a morally plausible institutional response to the crisis of disease and death.

So far this book has not attended directly to the covenantal image in an institutional setting. At a minimum, a covenantal ethic must reckon with the responsibilities not only of individual practitioners but also of the institutions for which they work, and it must deal with the complexities of making good on that covenant in a highly structured institutional framework that requires cooperation among a variety of professionals. I do not intend in the following to suggest that a covenantal ethic offers a unique solution to the problems and conflicts that emerge in the institutions that deliver health care. A covenant enjoins good-faith efforts that do not reduce to a casuistical system or to a single, preferred institutional design. But the attempt to keep faith institutionally ought, at the least, to free us to face candidly the tensions and conflicts that emerge in an institutional setting; and many of those conflicts can be explored by examining the marks of the so-called large-scale organization today, of which the hospital is but one instance.

## The Bureaucracy

It would take a very large institution to house all the literature generated on the subject of the large-scale organization. Nevertheless, the literature describes a few features that provide a convenient basis for ethical analysis. Large organizations usually define themselves by a single, stated primary mission (health, education, or the sale of products for profit). Furthermore, they have three structural characteristics: (1) They are hierarchically articulated into levels of super- and subordination; (2) they are internally differentiated into functions that require regular procedures and standards from department to department; (3) they emphasize the official and the impersonal at the expense of the personal.

Large-scale organizations can deviate from these characteristics. They can develop complex primary ends (the university teaching hospital simultaneously heals, teaches, and sponsors medical research; the conglomerate spans a number of businesses); but this complexity usually serves a single, inclusive primary aim (health or economic performance at a profit). Furthermore, the pyramidal structure of the corporation can be flat or steep; it can also decentralize to accommodate the work of specialized teams; but even the decentralized large-scale institution does not altogether dispense with hierarchy and routine. Finally, it may attempt to personalize service and humanize the work environment, but because it serves categories and masses, it cannot dispense altogether with impersonal standards of treatment and behavior. Some deviation exists—the marks of the large-scale organization are hardly indelible; but they persist enough to justify directing moral reflection to them.

## Primary Institutional Purpose

Large-scale organizations must be morally clear about their basic mission. They emerge, in the first place, in complex societies that have undergone considerable differentiation, and therefore specialization, of function. To serve the society well, they must perform well this primary function. The university must educate and the hospital must heal. Each has its institutional commitment and covenant, as it were. The university—or the hospital—cannot afford to be distracted by any and all extraneous goals. It must carefully ensure that secondary purposes—whether contributory, instrumental, incidental, or covert—do not supplant its primary purposes.

Some of the central images treated in this work mischievously bend health care institutions in some direction other than the primary task of healing. The military image subverts the primary end of health to a subordinate and merely *contributory* purpose: the fight against death. The image of the physician as technician elevates a merely *instrumental* good to a final good. To the degree, moreover, that the institution indulges the professional's pleasure in technical performance, it substitutes the *incidental* good of virtuosity for the overarching aim of medicine, all at the expense of what John Cheever called "that vast population of the comatose and the dying . . . kept alive, unconsciously, through trailblazing medical invention."[1]

The parental image, meanwhile, tends to substitute somewhat *covert* purposes for the primary end of a health care institution. The hospital exists to provide more care than the single practitioner and the family can deliver in the patient's home. But covertly, the hospital and staff also function as rubber gloves to insulate the society from the shock of disease and death. In a sense, these institutions perform a paternalistic function, not simply for inmates but for the society at large. Clearly, the total institution tends to handle inmates paternalistically: It deprives them of freedom for their own good. But at a deeper level, the institution also provides a protective, parental service for the society at large in sequestering the elderly, the disabled, and the infirm. Sometimes we do not want to handle the stricken because we cannot handle ourselves before them, and so we turn not only them but, in a sense, an unmastered portion of ourselves into the hands of the professionals.

A covenantal tradition, for reasons already developed in an earlier chapter, would define the primary purpose of health care institutions as just that—health care. Other goals—the prevention of death, protection against suffering, professional self-fulfillment, and provision of institutional respite from the burdens of care—should remain contributory, instrumental, incidental, and subordinate to the primary goal. But only communities a little less fearful of death are free to organize the profession and its institutions around strategies to fight or avoid suffering and death and thus are able to accept the more finite goal of health care.

A delivery system, moreover, that fixes on health and healing as its primary purpose will force a reassessment of hospital policies. We have already noted that once medicine no longer aims at death prevention alone, hospitals begin to distinguish between maximal treatment and optimal care. More teaching of patients will occur for the sake of effective preventive, rehabilitative, and chronic care. Perhaps also more hospitals will hire salaried professionals. Fee-for-service (or piecework) medicine feeds extravagantly off the fear of disease and death. The psychological mechanisms of unconditional resistance and avoidance push up health care costs when the primary goal of medicine fades.

The emphasis so far has fallen on the primary purpose of the health care institution, but this primary mission admits of some internal complexity. The large hospital simultaneously heals patients, conducts research, and teaches young residents and nurses. Although the purposes all converge on the goal of better health care at the distance of infinity, they also produce conflicts and conflicts of interest in the immediate present. The physician feels the strain of multiple institutional identities and loyalties. In a case appropriately dubbed "The Psychiatrist as Double Agent,"[2] Willard Gaylin and Daniel Callahan commented on a practitioner at a medical school whose diagnosis (latent schizophrenia) of a student on medical leave led to an eventual refusal of readmission. What does a psychiatrist owe to his patient by way of confidentiality? What does he owe to the university that employs him and to patients whom this physician-to-be might treat? The problem of the double agent, of course, confronts the physician in many other situations uncomplicated by the special obligations of employee to employer. Whom does the physician serve when experimenting on human subjects—the patient or medical progress? Whom, when screening and counseling in genetics—the needs and desires of the family or some vision the physician has of the genetic future of the human race? Whom, when drugging the hyperactive child—the child or the teacher in a large school system? Whom, when delivering health care at a teaching hospital—the patient as the object of therapy or the medical students whom the patient serves as teaching material? Whom, when committing the disturbed—the patient or the convenience of the family and the society? The psychiatrist, perhaps more than any other physician, faces problems in double agentry. The psychiatrist has often functioned as a gatekeeper in a special kind of incarceration. When no clear-cut therapeutic intent marks the patient's commitment, the physician becomes something other than a physician: a custodian, a baby-sitter, a jailer, a predictor of behavior, but not a caretaker and healer.

Other professions face the problem of double agentry. Just as research tempts the physician to use patients experimentally in ways that otherwise, as a pure therapist, he or she would not, so a cause may tempt a lawyer to develop a high-risk argument on behalf of a client, not because it serves the client's best interests, but because the argument might yield for the lawyer and the lawyer's cause a landmark decision. Mindful of this temptation, the Code of Professional Responsibility in the legal profession prohibits the lawyer from being "more concerned with the establishment or extension of legal principles than in the immediate protection of the rights of the lawyer's individual client."[3] Regulations governing experimentation on human subjects push health care institutions toward the same priorities in favor of patient care over the more remote goals of medical discovery.

In addition to this complexity and tension in responsibilities that develop as medicine pursues its primary end, health care institutions face further secondary responsibilities as public or quasi-public institutions. What special obligations should they fulfill to the neighborhoods and communities around them? Hospitals in urban areas especially need to face this question. When the city about them deteriorates, they fulfill their primary functions only with difficulty. Corporations, universities, and hospitals eventually suffer if, although giants in their fields, they pose as social and political nonentities and let the cities around them fall to pieces. The ghetto hospital mentioned earlier survived considerable turbulence because its home care service had earned the respect of its neighbors.

The sheer size of our great institutions gives a public scope and dignity to the lives of those who work for them. It bestows a public meaning on the lives of their workers, which draws the latter out of a cramped privacy. At the same time, this grandeur creates two problems. It can obscure for participants the fact that the institution's imperatives do not exhaust the meaning of public responsibility, that the institution must take its place within the still-larger framework of the society as a whole and its common good. Health, although a fundamental human good, constitutes only one good among others and not the highest at that. Neither professionals nor the institutions for which they work have a moral warrant in a health-obsessed age to bloat this good beyond its place in human affairs.

Furthermore, the sheer size and grandeur of the institution sometimes draw workers into making the intramural life of the institution an end in itself. An academician once commented in the faculty tearoom during a vacation break: "This is a delicious place without the students." Professionals at work in large institutions often take themselves and their transactions with colleagues more seriously than their dealings with those they serve, a fact that returns us to our baseline in covenantal thought.

Institutions, consciously or unconsciously, embody a covenant, a social purpose, a human good, which they avow and serve. And in the course of rendering that service, institutions receive as well as give to the community. At one time, hospitals, largely charitable (in the sense of philanthropic institutions), perceived themselves as givers alone (although the poor often had to consent to experimentation to receive care). Under a third-party payment system, the buying and selling of the marketplace has largely replaced the philanthropic ideal of giving. The managers of a modern hospital think in massively contractual terms. But beneath the massive selling of services and the token philanthropies lies a covenantal base of giving and receiving that ought to infuse it. The community, after all, charters its life, grants it protection, and endows its enterprises with a public significance to which it must respond.

## The Hierarchical versus the Collegial

The hierarchical structure of the large-scale organization conflicts with the natural mode of organization among professionals, which is collegial. Historically, professionals have accepted patterns of super- and subordination among themselves only as temporary phases of training and education. The apprentice serves a master only because he or she has not yet become a full-fledged professional and therefore a colleague. In attaining professional status, the apprentice acquires an independent relation to sources of knowledge and accumulates sufficient experience to apply this knowledge to specific cases. This direct access that each professional has to the knowledge base on which the profession rests logically led to the professional ideal of independence. Professionals are educated rather than merely trained; that is, they have a direct grasp of first principles. This bestows on them the mark of independence. The principle of collegiality expresses this independence in a community of professionals; colleagues ideally act in concert with one another chiefly by persuasion rather than command.

A hierarchically ordered institution, on the other hand, indulges in leadership by persuasion (teaching) but finally rests on command and on sanctions vested in that command. Professionals thus face, in principle at least, serious potential conflicts between the imperatives of the organization and those derived from the aims and purposes of the profession. A bureaucracy subordinates them; their profession may demand, awkwardly enough, insubordination. The conflict goes deeper than the occasional overt crisis when the professional must "blow the whistle." The collegial and the bureaucratic types of social organization establish somewhat conflicting modes of social identity and duty, which one and the same person may suffer unresolved.

However, administrators of the hierarchical organization do not make satisfactory villains and even deserve some sympathy. Administrators must function in a culture that is hierarchical and bureaucratic to the hilt and yet suspicious of bureaucracy. Administrators today hardly enjoy great honor or power or tangible satisfaction. Our society gossips about them more than it honors them; it lets them wield the appearance more than the substance of power; it sandwiches them in the hierarchy somewhere between the ham and the hard cheese and deprives them of the tangible satisfactions of curing a single patient. Their one indisputable value to other professionals lies in reminding them of how fortunate they are not to be administrators.

Our large-scale institutions create two kinds of administrators: those who move into administration out of the ranks of the medical profession and those who have no such credentials but who have made a profession of administration.

Physicians who stray into administration have both advantages and disadvantages. To their advantage, they know the profession, as it were, from the ground up. This special knowledge and experience usually qualify them symbolically for the top job as head of a health care institution. Yet at the same time, physician-administrators are uncomfortable, amphibious creatures. They have not moved so far into administration as to lose their identity as physicians, but they have moved too far into it to make good on that identity. Psychologically, physician-administrators occupy a kind of no-man's-land between two worlds. To keep up their professional identity, they find themselves living off the capital of their education and experience; but gradually the neglect of their continuing professional education catches up with them, and they feel "out of it." Professionally, they resemble somewhat-deteriorated university buildings subjected to deferred maintenance. For the good of an institution and its leadership, regular furloughs may be a sound investment.

Full-time managers, on the other hand, have not gone through the special training of the professionals on their own staff; they usually have a specialized professional training of their own in business schools, schools of public administration, or more specialized university settings in health care administration.

Administrators, whether or not they have a medical background, differ functionally from hands-on professionals. Categories helpful in stating the difference surfaced in Chapter 1, on the physician as parent. The Columbia historian Walter P. Metzger, following the sociologist Georg Simmel, has distinguished between three types of human relationships, all of them asymmetrical.[4] Each entails an imbalance in the relationship between a superordinate and a subordinate.

In the first type, the superordinate acts on *his or her own behalf* and at the expense of the subordinate. This type exploits; the exploitation can be overt, as in the case of slavery, or masked, as in the case of the bad parent who pretends concern for the child while exercising authority for his or her own benefit. In the second type, the superordinate acts on behalf of the welfare of the subordinate. This person acts benevolently, paternalistically, and professionally when solving a practical problem that a patient or client faces. A professional exercises this kind of authority as a lawyer, physician, surgeon, accountant, minister, priest, or rabbi. Finally, the superordinate may act primarily for the sake of the institution to which they both belong. This is the managerial mode of authority, and it finds its natural habitat in the bureaucracy.

Metzger's functional types help to clarify the difference between the hands-on professional and the professional manager. Clearly, the manager must plan for the well-being of workers and staff members under his or her charge, but the relationship of super- and subordination does not exist—at least not primarily—for that purpose. It orients to the well-being of the institution from which their own welfare mediately derives. Just as clearly, however, the manager cannot treat the institution as a client: The institution is hardly subordinate to the manager as superordinate. The administrator *belongs to* the institution even when he or she occupies a position of top management and control. A close identity with the enterprise makes it harder for the manager to maintain a measure of independence, whether psychological or moral, from the institution and its imperatives.

The contrast in the sheer length of case studies in the field of medicine and management symbolizes the difference between the professional and the manager. When physicians prepared cases for a summer seminar I taught in medical ethics, their case write-ups were remarkably terse. Doctors usually have the patient dead by page two. When managers, however, presented cases for a seminar in management ethics that I taught, I found myself dealing with a manuscript the bulk of a *New Yorker* essay (in length if not in elegance)—fifty to seventy-five pages. This difference in length symbolizes an important difference in the moral problems each profession faces. The doctor may have dozens or hundreds of patients. The fact of sheer numbers allows for—and demands—some distance from each. Indeed, the physician faces some of the problems of callused detachment. But the administrator must live, breathe, worry, conspire, and aspire largely in the confines of the single institution for which he or she works. It envelops the administrator. It becomes his or her de facto world. This psychological envelopment does not confer upon managers the right to abandon either general moral constraints or the special constraints that managers as a professional class may see fit to accept for themselves. But it does mean that moral purposes must be largely built into the very structure of the institution. Management must oversee this task of moral construction. It cannot depend on the fitful efforts of individual persons alone to keep covenant.

## The Bureaucratic Emphasis on the Technical

Routinized bureaucratic organization also affects the professional aspiration to excellence. The large-scale organization offers a mechanism whereby people can accomplish great things without themselves being great. The corporation depends on efficient routines rather than heroics and charisma for its stability and growth. In a sense, the professions fit into this process of routinization. The very existence of the professions guarantees standards—for the selection of candidates to be trained, for educational experience, and for performance. These standards, for the most part, protect the laity from exposure to erratic and idiosyncratic treatment, whether at the hand of genius or fraud.

As professionals move into large-scale organizations, they reinforce routinization, and, on the positive side, make it somewhat easier to enforce minimum standards. (The solo practitioner can largely escape the scrutiny of colleagues, whereas the teaching hospital can more easily monitor the work of its staff members.) Unfortunately, the large-scale organization can also flatten out the aspiration to excellence in its diverse forms. Predictable routines for handling cases work more conveniently in an institution than do bold and singular responses to assignments. Minimal standards sometimes provide a very low ceiling that attracts the uninspired to that level of performance and no more. Legislative sanction becomes a double-edged sword in the course of litigation; it cuts out the grossly incompetent but also protects the jobs of the mediocre. And when the bureaucracy presses for excellence, it tends to opt for its most technical and measurable forms.

These difficulties that the large-scale organization of professionals faces in maintaining its drive for excellence argue for critical reflection and experiment with alternative modes of organization, but they do not persuade one to join the nostalgic who yearn for the days of the freelance entrepreneur, the private practitioner. The nineteenth-century liberal myth saw people as better in isolation than in society. Even the realistic Reinhold Niebuhr fell prey to liberal innocence when he titled his work *Moral Man and Immoral Society*. Men and women need community, not merely for the instrumental purpose of producing greater things than they can achieve by themselves, but for the moral reason of helping them to be better than they can be by themselves. One does not have to be a Puritan to respect the truth in the opposite: Immoral Man and Moral Society. Men and women need the support, correction, and encouragement of their fellows, and physicians are no exception.

But this line of argument demands that institutions cultivate and prize more than technical competence. Specifically, they must prize some of the virtues that certain others of the images foster: the compassion and donative spirit of the parent, the fidelity of the covenant partner in health care, the clarity, imagination, and patience of the good teacher, the discipline of the first-rate military leader. Here our universities and churches bear a major responsibility. As the institution that trains the modern professional, the university has done a brilliant job of equipping the professional with technical competence, but it has not always accepted responsibility for nourishing that moral substance and cultivating those virtues that a society has a right to expect in professionals. The church and synagogue, as institutions that provide spiritual incentive for at least some members of the professional community, and that started and—for a while at least—financially contributed to many of our hospitals, have, unconscionably, faded from the scene, except for only-too-often marginal and ineffectual chaplaincy programs. They have raised no searching questions about the ethos and commitments of those institutions in which so many people face their most crisis-laden days.

## The Impersonal versus the Personal

The bureaucratic emphasis on the office, rather than the person, creates difficulties for physicians and administrators in three directions: It produces conflicts with duties to patients, to oneself, and to colleagues.

Patients acutely sense the deprivations that result from official, officious, and impersonal treatment. Tolstoy's Ivan Ilych put it most trenchantly:

> There was the usual waiting and the important air assumed by the doctor with which he was so familiar (resembling that which he himself assumed in court). . . . To Ivan Ilych only one question was important: was his case serious or not? But the doctor ignored that inappropriate question. From his point of view it was not the one under consideration, the real question was to decide between a floating kidney, chronic catarrh or appendicitis. It was not a question of life or death, but one between a floating kidney and appendicitis.[5]

Dealing in huge numbers and attempting to deal fairly combine to force the large organization to deal impersonally. Patients, clients, and consumers complain of impersonal treatment, and the existentialists developed this complaint into a broadside against modern mass society. They bemoaned a culture that reduces subjects to objects, persons to things. The manager symbolizes this reduction, for the very term "manager," like "manipulation," derives from the Latin word for hands; the manager "handles" others, a mode of relationship that has less to do with the personal predilections and sensitivity of the manager than with the very structure and scale of the institution.

This criticism has an important element of truth. The ideal physician should not simply treat the disease but reckon with the patient. The failure to do so in the large-scale organization has led to the exploration of significant alternatives and supplements to the prevailing health care system: the self-care movement, the hospice movement, and the holistic health care movement.

Within limits, sensitive administrators and professionals working in a bureaucracy can lean against some of its tendencies toward institutional callousness. Some reforms, particularly in the allocation of time to patients and in the training of residents, help considerably to give the hospital a "human face." But some superficial efforts at "personalizing" relationships only remind the inmate of the highly impersonal environment that engulfs a person there. "Personalizing" relationships smacks too much of Sanforizing pants. The very process industrializes intimacy. Physicians, managers, and administrators must also accept without false dismay the incompleteness of their contacts with those over whom they exercise control. In doing their limited jobs, they often serve persons well whose fellowship, in personal terms, they will never enjoy.

The organizational emphasis on the impersonal rather than the personal runs a second danger of impoverishing the self that fills the office; it conflicts with one's duties to oneself. The careerist totally subordinates himself or herself to the office and becomes, in the course of time, a cipher, a spectral being, deferring satisfactions and evading pain by referring it from its deeper psychic levels to petty frustrations. Such a person becomes guilty of what Nietzsche called the "work neurosis." The "now" generation criticized such careerism for its tunnel vision; Jungians took it to task for its one-sidedness. Careerism prefers the *animus* to the *anima*, the rational to the affective, the manipulative to the sensitive, and thereby diminishes the self. Resentful spouses, broken marriages, alienated children, drug addiction, early health problems, and career burnout reflect this psychic disarray. Wrongly interpreted, a covenantal ethic appears to contribute to a self-consuming, eventually destructive commitment. As stated earlier, the notion of covenant cuts deeper into personal identity than either a limited contractual or a technical interpretation of professional duty. But I also noted earlier that the biblical notion of covenant produces an inner freedom and nonchalance that make a deeper commitment to others tolerable. The religious tradition imparts a sense of the final extraterritoriality of the person that makes it possible to function in a "hardship post," as it were, without being annihilated thereby. One can take a job seriously precisely because one does not take it too seriously. It has not become the sole arena of self-realization. One can also accept the lesser distinctions between the office and the person without finding them disconcertingly schizophrenic. Official roles and social masks do not necessarily impoverish or stifle the agent who must play and wear them. On the contrary, they provide the self with a social fig leaf; they permit some measure of personal life to thrive behind them.

Finally, the bureaucratic emphasis on the impersonal at the expense of the personal presents difficulties, especially for Americans, in dealings with colleagues. American professionals find themselves caught between the pressure of a social structure that is highly formal, bureaucratic, and competitive—energized throughout by the rewards of promotion—and a social style predicated on friendliness, informality, and intimacy as its ideal. The impersonal strains against the personal; the hierarchical against the egalitarian; and the competitive against the impulse to help others. The resultant moral conflicts between loyalty to the institution and loyalty to friends can be immense.

Some societies protect their members from such conflicts by separating the public order of work from the private order of friendship. But Americans peculiarly combine these orders at the risk of corrupting them both. Caught between the demands of an impersonal social system and a social style in which friendliness counts for so much, Americans carry a heavy burden of guilt over betrayal of the friend or compromise of the institution. They make friends at work, but then find themselves making professional judgments and decisions about those befriended. The confidences of friendship inspire some measure of personal loyalty, but they also render two people more vulnerable to each other in their weaknesses. The course of friendship reveals secrets and confidences. But then it can happen that a man finds himself suddenly called upon to judge impersonally those in whom he has confided and who have confided in him. Uncomfortably, he helps turn them over to the machinery of the system—not entirely certain that the system itself hands out justice as it reviews the individual case. Moreover, friendship in the bureaucratic setting has its darker side. Irrespective of the formal table of organization, staff members polarize into shifting patterns of friendship and enmity. It becomes even more difficult to make unclouded professional judgments about colleagues adversarially defined.

The social mobility of Americans increases the competitive tension throughout the system. The social system lacks a ceiling above and a floor below. Thus, the rewards for backbiting can tempt; the threat of the betrayal by others can chill. Under these circumstances, the prevailing social style remains outwardly friendly and direct; but inwardly a wariness takes possession of the soul and corrodes the workplace with distrust.

It must be frankly conceded that covenantal obligations to friends and institutions can conflict. But the earlier discussion of professional self-regulation makes it clear why the heavier accent must fall on obligations to the institution—as defined by professional purpose. The immense powers professionals wield, in and out of the institutional setting, and the fateful consequences of their actions for patients forbid the professional to warp judgment for reasons of friendship. This does not mean that a covenantal ethic depresses altogether the claims of friendship or obligations to one's colleagues. The chief obstacle to friendship comes not from conflicting institutional obligations but from a careerist preoccupation with one's self. The word "career" perhaps not accidentally derives from the same root as "car," in our culture a self-driven vehicle. Today a vocation deteriorates only too often into a career that is a kind of self-driven vehicle through life, that deals expediently with both institutions and friends in the nervous effort to get ahead. Rightly understood, a covenantal ethic should help strengthen both institutional and collegial ties.

## Beyond the Hospital

Reforms of hospitals are in order—to orient them better toward their appointed goals and to lessen structural conflicts or to allow those conflicts to surface in more constructive ways. At the same time, experiments in the health care delivery system beyond the walls of the hospital make sense. We may be moving toward a period of duplex social organization in which we require both large-scale institutions, with the resources they can mobilize, and smaller, more informal communities, delivering services that supplement and experiment in ways unavailable to huge, more cumbersome institutions. Living as we do in the "age of the organization," we cannot expect any and all of these experiments to remain small. Nor should they, as long as the society remains open to fresh experiment. We also should not expect such experiments to depend entirely on small, informal communities for their support. Some may depend on voluntary communities—service organizations, churches, and synagogues—for their support. Others depend on corporations. Still others need federal support or some mix of all three.

None of the movements mentioned is unknown to the reader. In one way or another, they all embody efforts to limit the acute care hospital as the single, imperial institution in the health care system.

The hospice, for example, can, in some cases, care for the dying much more aptly than can the hospital, that is, if terminal care aims at healing (in the sense of "making whole"). The dying need not more life but more healing in the midst of dying. Patients may remain much more integral and whole before the crisis of death in the hospice or in their homes as assisted by the resources of a hospice. The movement received its chief impetus in this country largely from religiously committed people. It needs, however, federal funding, which it has had difficulty in securing despite the cost-competitive services it offers.

Health maintenance organizations, at their best, attempt to shift the emphasis in health care away from acute care toward better preventive, rehabilitative, and chronic care, by giving participating doctors financial incentives to keep their HMO patients well. Although the early growth of HMOs depended on corporate support (e.g., from the various Kaiser companies), more recently they have enjoyed substantial federal subsidy.

HMOs face substantial problems. They attract a disproportionate number of early subscribers with multiple and expensive health problems. They have not solved the problem of the so-called worried well patient who places excessive demands on resources. Although their use of largely salaried professionals helps reduce the cost of physician care, they rarely own their own hospitals. Thus convenient access to hospitals and institutional cost-containment are hard to achieve. Patients complain of the impersonality of care. HMOs accommodate to provide personal, continuous care to a patient if the patient makes advance appointments, but obviously an HMO cannot automatically provide such continuity as would be forthcoming in a visit to a physician's private office. In two respects, the reliance on financial incentives to reduce health costs (physicians participate in a bonus system) does not wholly solve the problem. First, the 30 percent turnover in patients in a given year means that the HMO in question does not reap the reward for better health even if it has been achieved. Second, financial incentives alone do not substitute for a professional dedication and an institutional commitment that partly impelled the movement in the first place. These very considerable difficulties, however, do not constitute reasons for abandoning the experiment with HMOs. They represent an important alternative to the current system to help keep it more competitive and an important effort to shift the accent away from acute care.

Neighborhood health clinics play a similarly important role in outpatient care. They work especially well if they understand neighborhood values and have people who can speak the language of the residents. The efficiency of such clinics shows not in the number of patients processed but in end results: the improvement of health in the neighborhood served. Unfortunately, the fee-for-service system rewards means (speed in processing patients) rather than ends (actual improvements in health). Marna Carney, an economist, has uncovered various statistically demonstrable benefits from the work of neighborhood clinics (which she compared with similar neighborhoods unserved by clinics): (1) a decline in rheumatic fever, (2) reduced hospitalization, (3) lower health care costs, (4) better yields in preventive medicine, (5) improved general health.[6] The holistic health care movement and organized efforts at self-care represent further experiments today. The first enjoys some support from official religious traditions; the second, in its more zealous, narcissistic forms, offers a kind of substitute for religion. I do not have the competence to assess these movements in their variety. But the holistic health care movement relies heavily on the work of a health care team, in this instance not the conventional team that works in a hospital setting but one that includes, as well, the minister-priest. It bids fair to raise the question of whether professionals in concert with patients can restore healing to a religious context—for it is into such a context that healers from the shaman to the Hippocratic physician, among others in the Western tradition, quietly but persistently have put it.

This brief comment about movements and experiments beyond the compass of the acute-care hospital does not close with a proposal for its eclipse or with a prayer for a yet-uninvented saving alternative. I would not want to argue with the romantics of the 1960s in favor of dismantling the bureaucracies. They can mobilize equipment and professional talent and effect some economies of scale available under no other institutional form. The increased role of other institutions and movements should not mean the decline of the hospital, but rather a recognition of its "cathedral" or "mother ship" responsibilities to other institutions, once it gets its own priorities in hand.

## The Health Care Team

Whether in a hospital setting or not, the health care team today is pivotal in the delivery of health care; it looms large in group practice, the clinic, the holistic health care movement, as well as the hospital service. The importance of that team reminds us that covenantal responsibility is not merely individual or institutional but depends also on the commitment of a small community of healers working together, most often in a hierarchical organization.

Whatever the setting, ways must be found to help teams work more flexibly and collegially. Perhaps we have too narrowly restricted the models for defining interprofessional relationships. We prize, on the one hand, a peculiar form of the ideal of teamwork that discourages all discussion of alternatives and criticism of ends and emphasizes the purely secondary and instrumental virtues of cooperativeness. Meanwhile we activate, on the other hand, a somewhat more adversarial, contentious ideal. We anticipate the failure to agree on ends and react to this failure by becoming hypersensitive about procedures and privileges. Ironically, even opponents of bureaucracies who work for bureaucracies help them grow by proliferating red tape to protect themselves from colleagues within its walls. Collaboration between professionals differs from teamwork among technicians: It must find ways of allowing substantive differences about ends to surface without destroying through criticism the communal basis for judgment and action.

The physician still remains the key to the achievement of teamwork. Partly in recognition of that fact, this book, although about the healer, deals chiefly with the physician. I make no apologies for this emphasis, inasmuch as the physician wields immense power and creates the central problem in the healing enterprise. Yet healing is a communal activity. Covenant commits more than the individual. God makes his covenant with Abraham, but through that covenant God brings into being a covenanted community that shoulders responsibility as a servant community to others. Otherwise, covenant deteriorates into the commitment of the loner, the physician as solitary gunslinger. But if healing reflects the work of a healing community—the social worker, the nurse, the physical therapist, the hospital chaplain, the patient, and, in varying degrees and serendipitously, friends, relatives, and "significant others" in the patient's life—then we must close with the physician's potential conflicts and tensions with other professionals on the health care team.

The physician develops a primary professional identity through a specialized skill—as oncologist, pediatrician, psychiatrist, or surgeon. As such, he or she serves as a member of a health care team; each member has specialized tasks to perform. But at the same time a doctor often functions as the executive *head* of that team. The doctor enjoys that authority— at least over other nonmedical professionals—on the strength of that special skill. Consequently, the physician plays two roles: first violinist and conductor of the orchestra. As specialist, the physician works as a *part* of the whole; but as head of the team, the physician makes each part a shadow of his or her leadership, a partial extension and implementation of his or her strategies. As specialist, the physician must target technical services to meet an aspect of the patient's needs—must treat the disease. But as director of the health care team, the physician must attend to the whole needs of the patient.

But there's the rub; it is difficult, under the best of circumstances, to be both first violinist and conductor of the orchestra, quarterback and coach, pitcher and manager of the team. Large corporations recognize this. Members of top management do not usually administer specialized functions in the organization. The roles of top policymaker and specialist conflict. If a person gets trapped with both responsibilities, he or she usually attends to one at the expense of the other. This happens with particular ease in a hospital setting; the technical gets emphasized at the expense of the directorial, the disease at the expense of the person who is its host.

This particular resolution leads increasingly to conflicts with the nursing staff. Modern nurses step in with a somewhat different view of their role than the one the physician maps out for them. They do not think of themselves as merely implementers of the physician's strategy. Only too often, the strategist, preoccupied with his or her own work as a specialist, lets the comprehensive strategy lie undeveloped. The first violinist plays too busily to orchestrate the whole. Increasingly, nurses define their responsibility as care for the whole person. That broadening of responsibility, however, puts them in an awkward position. It implies the reduction of the doctor to a rather subordinate role. Nurses aspire to a role and responsibility without the power of command that it requires. They must operate behind the scenes, conducting an orchestra without any control whatsoever over the first violinist. Their new perception of themselves has no public status.

Experience as an observer at a psychiatric hospital several years ago led me to the conclusion that psychiatrists and nurses on psychiatric units have a better modus operandi than one finds elsewhere in medicine. On the whole, they found it more natural to work collaboratively. In the first place, the very nature of psychiatric problems requires that the psychiatrist attend to the total pattern of a patient's response. The physician must take seriously his or her role as director of the health care team. Second, the special needs of psychiatric diagnosis, monitoring, and treatment involve the nurse and others in a more active, collaborative role. A specialist in internal medicine can often bypass the testimony of the nurse on the floor to get the information he or she wants from X rays, lab tests, and charts. But the psychiatrist, in addition to these impersonal sources, needs the nurse's testimony about patient behavior in assessing both the problem and the effectiveness of therapy. Moreover, the psychiatric nurse's attitude toward a treatment plan, including such items as weekend furloughs, can affect the plan's success.

These impressions, if correct, suggest that the health care team can have a director and still grant to other members of the health care team an active, collaborative role. The image of the orchestral performance, however, suggests that the team cannot broker power and authority crudely. The successful performance, after all, requires that the conductor, first violinist, and last-row timpanist alike subordinate themselves to the score.

But to attend faithfully to the score, professionals need more than policy guidelines and correct institutional procedures. Fidelity to the patient and the patient's plight requires a brace of personal virtues, apart from which high-strung professionals will find it difficult to make a specific system work. At a minimum, these virtues include a measure of charity and good faith in dealing with an irritating colleague; a good dose of caution in heeding a friend who only too quickly approves what we have to say; humility before the powers we wield for good or for ill; the discipline to seek wisdom rather than show off by scoring points; sufficient integrity not to pretend to more certainty than we have; and enough bravery to act when we must, even in the midst of uncertainty. These are some of the virtues that make sense in those who aspire to a corrective vision yet must reckon with the fact that they see through a glass darkly.

*Chapter Seven*

# A Covenanted
# Health Care System

C ovenanted physicians and covenanted hospitals
cannot fully sustain themselves or their mission
on their own without a health care system that reflects
a covenantal sense of responsibility. Nonprofit as well
as for-profit hospitals face the pressures of the bottom
line: One worries about profits; the other about
survival. Both, under current systemic conditions,
threaten to squeeze the air out of what healers are
called to profess. The dramatic unfolding events of
the 1990s have made that ringingly clear. The Clin-
tons broached the issue of health care reform in 1993.
Doctors and patients alike worried about seismic
changes in health care issuing from Washington, but
the truly revolutionary changes occurred below the
radar screen in Louisville, Kentucky, and Nashville,
Tennessee, the homes of the huge prepayment systems that under managed care rapidly began to
replace fee-for-service medicine. The Clinton pro-
posals failed, but the basic problem of sustaining an
equitable health care system will not go away. Even
insurance agents recognize today that the number of
Americans without health care insurance and coverage is rapidly rising again.

## The Problem

Our health care system contains much that we should be proud of and much that we should conserve. It has enlisted the devotion of millions of health care professionals, created splendid hospitals, clinics, and research institutions, and dazzled the world with its technical achievements. And it has allowed for some choice in doctors. Any reform of the system must preserve its virtues.

Yet our health care system is seriously flawed. It fails to reach many of us: At any given time, it excludes over one-seventh of Americans (about 43 million people) from health care insurance; it leaves another one-seventh underinsured. The consequences for individuals and families are devastating. When we exclude people from health care, they suffer a triple deprivation—the pain of illness, the desperation of little or no treatment, and the cruel proof that they do not really belong to the community. We make them strangers and sojourners in their own land.

When we do not give access to care, we also diminish the vigor of our common life. Sick people cannot work productively. In relieving individual, private distress, a nation enables its people to contribute more fully to public life and to economic well-being. Thereby the nation serves its own public flourishing, not only instrumentally but also morally and psychologically to the degree that it signals by its care the strength of its covenant with its own.

Our system also does not offer enough primary, preventive, home, and long term-care; and it woefully neglects mental health coverage. We tend to be acute care gluttons and preventive care anemics.

Reflecting its lopsided emphasis on acute care, the system oversupplies us with specialists (some 70 percent of our doctors are specialists, compared with only 30 to 50 percent in comparable industrial countries) and undersupplies us with generalists whom we need for effective preventive, rehabilitative, and long-term care.

The system pays for procedures contracted for and performed; it does not provide enough incentives for good health outcomes achieved; and it exposes those who cannot pay to dramatically lower success rates for a given procedure. It often overtreats; yet insurance sometimes deserts when most needed. It can expose the person who has lost his or her job to financial ruin. It locks others with pre-existing conditions into jobs they do not want; and the system often establishes lifetime limits on care.

The system burdens health care practitioners and institutions with too many regulations and forms. A financial officer at one hospital reports that her staff has to handle more than three thousand different types of accounts receivable. The head of the major county hospital in Dallas, Texas says that he needs a staff of three hundred people to handle what, at a comparable hospital under the Canadian system, three people dispatch handily.

Our system also costs more to operate than any other health care system in the world; no other country spends more than 10 percent of its GNP for health care, yet we are above 14 percent and if we maintain the current level of care, costs will rise still further. The system now consumes one-seventh of everything that we make or do. Even this figure does not fully measure the cost. The "fringe benefit" of health care is anything but a fringe cost of producing cars, computers, refrigerators, and, for that matter, education. In some of our industries, health benefits cost more than anything except wages and salaries. This cost reduces the competitiveness of plant locations in the United States: Why should companies build cars in Detroit if their health care costs per worker are $500 to $750 less across the bridge in Windsor, Canada? Some commentators have argued that we have recently slowed down the increasing costs of medical care. But under three presidents, we have undergone temporary slowdowns in costs, only to see them speed up again. For our own sake and the sake of our children, we must be better stewards of our nation's resources.

Furthermore, our payment system is unfair. Businesses, insurance companies, hospitals, the government, and patients furiously shift costs as they fob off their expenses on others. Hospitals jack up their prices to the insured to cover their costs in caring for indigent patients. Some doctors try to skim off well-insured patients, while rejecting others. Insurance companies sift for healthy customers to avoid payouts to the sick. Companies shift to part-time, temporary, or younger employees to reduce health insurance costs. The government's savings on Medicare and Medicaid patients sometimes come at the expense of prices paid by insured patients. Some people are forced to stay on welfare because the low-paying jobs in the service industries do not provide the health insurance they receive under Medicaid. All this artful dodging eventually dumps costs on workers and tax payers, through lower salary raises, higher taxes, or higher insurance payments.

## Ethical Foundations

A major reform of our health care system would rank as the most comprehensive piece of social legislation since the establishment of our social security system. We cannot engage in so grand an undertaking without being clear about its moral foundations. In my judgment, those foundations are three: *(1) Health care is a fundamental good; (2) health care is not the only fundamental good;* and *(3) health care is a public good.*

*1. Health care is a fundamental good* because it is one of the necessities of life. It is not an optional commodity, like a Walkman, a tie, or a scarf. Mothers instinctively affirm this truth when they concentrate their hopes on just this: the birth of a healthy baby—ten fingers, ten toes, a good heart, robust lungs. Why this single, humble, anxious wish? The mother prizes her baby's health because of the promise it holds for the child's life and flourishing. Healthy children, and therefore health care, are part of a nation's covenant with its future.

Because health care is a fundamental good, the American system must honor and reflect the following moral principles.

*The system must offer universal access.* Health benefits should reach all of us without financial or other barriers. Citizens should not fear that part-time or temporary employment, or a change or loss of a job, will cost them their health care. No one should lose access to health insurance because of pre-existing conditions, age, race, or genetic background. Barriers to access arising from linguistic and cultural differences, geographical distance, and disability must also come down.

Why should Americans especially insist that a basic good, such as health care, ought to reach all citizens? Our three major religious traditions—Protestant, Catholic, and Jewish—are communitarian. They all insist that we leave no one out in the cold when naked, starved, or sick.

Some individualists may counter that our revolutionary emphasis on individual liberty broke with this
communitarian religious heritage. This view of our
past, however, overlooks the first words we spoke as a
nation: "We, the people." The Preamble to the Constitution does not proclaim, "We, the factions of the
United States" or "We, the interest groups of the
United States" or "We, the individuals of the United
States," but "We, the people." That declaration was
tested and affirmed through the bitter ordeal of the
Civil War. We could not survive, half-slave, half-free.
Neither can we stand divided half-sick and half-well,
half-protected and half-uninsured. Our flourishing as
a people rests on our ability to create a health care system that binds us together as a nation. The principle
of universal access goes to the soul of reform. Currently, we are the only industrial nation, other than
South Africa, that fails to offer universal access.

*The system must be comprehensive.* Benefits must meet
the full range of health care needs. We should offer
primary, preventive, and some long-term care, as well
as acute care; home as well as hospital care; treatment
for mental as well as physical illness. An observer once
saw through our lopsided allocations in the United
States when he wrote, "Our system's philosophy might
be condensed in the motto, 'Millions for [acute] care
and not one cent for prevention!'" Those lines were
written in 1886. When we attend too little to primary,
preventive, and mental health care, the cost of acute
care increases; we mistarget funds; and we fail to help
people take responsibility for their own health.

When we do not offer comprehensive coverage, we
also fail to offer universal coverage. We discriminate
against whole classes of the afflicted, such as the mentally ill or those in need of long-term care. We would

find it strange to treat renal disease but not heart attack victims. But currently many plans lavish care on the physically ill but ignore the mentally ill. A scheme that aspires to universal coverage must offer a comprehensive package.

*The system must be fair.* It should not create a two-nation system—dividing the nation or the generations over this fundamental good. It should spread the costs and burdens of meeting our health care needs fairly, across the entire community.

Some might respond: Don't the uninsured receive the benefit of care through the emergency room? Unfortunately, their care does not match the care the insured receive. Their mortality rate for a given procedure is 1.8 times higher than the rate for the insured. The astronomical costs of some acute and long-term services can impoverish the sick and disabled and their families, and the prospect of these costs imperils the security of those of us who have not yet been stricken.

We would find it absurd to limit the protection of the Department of Defense—another fundamental good—to protecting only those who can afford a private army. We ought not limit access to medical care only to those who can hire a platoon of doctors.

We also need a system that fairly shares the cost of health care. We must secure contributions from all and eliminate the widespread patterns of cost shifting and free loading. A fair sharing of benefits and burdens draws the community together and ties the generations to one another.

*The system must be of high quality.* Health care is too important a good not to be good. Fostering good quality requires providing health care professionals with an environment that encourages their best work, protects the integrity of professional judgment, delivers effective treatments, and weeds out unethical and incompetent practitioners. It also means providing patients with sufficient information about the outcomes achieved by different plans to help them make informed, rational choices.

Ordinarily, consumers in the marketplace can enforce quality through their ability to compare products knowledgeably. But patients today do not have the information to make those judgments about doctors, hospitals, and health care plans—and it is difficult to acquire this knowledge in the midst of a medical crisis. Without the assurance of quality in the basic health care package, the well-to-do will buy up and out, returning the country to a two-nation health care system.

Health care is also too important a good not to get better. Therefore, the system must support research for improving the full range of health care services, including research on the outcomes of health care and more research directed to preventive, rehabilitative, and terminal care. We currently allocate almost all our research money to fight death, very little to ease pain and suffering for the living and dying.

*The system must be responsive to choice.* Health care is too fundamental a good, affecting each of us too intimately and fatefully, not to give us some measure of freedom to choose our doctors, the treatments we receive, and the health care plans in which we receive them. Too many people lack choice altogether or enjoy choice on only one of these matters. Honoring choice in the health care system not only respects liberty; it also engages the patient in the activity of preventive, acute, rehabilitative, and long-term care.

*2. Health care is not the only fundamental good.* We must also defend the nation, provide housing, and educate our children. Thus we need a system that allocates wisely and manages efficiently so that we can pay for these other basic goods.

To enable us to allocate wisely, the health care system must let us compare and balance what we spend on health care against other national priorities and evaluate and choose among diverse health services. In the past, the structure and funding of the health care system have not given us enough information about costs to make clear choices among these priorities. We need this information to put ourselves in a better position to meet all our other social needs and also to decide more wisely among competing health care needs.

Efficient and cost-effective management is a moral, not just an economic, imperative. Ethics is not one sphere and economics another. The British universities were right when they linked the study of economics, politics, and philosophy. Ethics, politics, and economics interconnect.

The health care system should also be simple to use without bureaucratic roadblocks that hinder the delivery of care. I have two daughters who are physicians, and they find it discouraging to talk to a person at the other end of an 800 line, someone who can approve or refuse a treatment, and who asks "How do you spell manic depressive?" Senator Robert Dole criticized the Clinton plan for its complexity by showing an organizational chart of the plan on TV: He did not mention that the current system is so complex that one could not even bring it into view on a TV camera. Nevertheless, Senator Dole had a point. Whatever the reform plan, it must offer simple access for patients and ease of management for doctors and other caregivers. The Clinton administration, sensitive to this need, sought to make provider organizations rather than a National Health Council or state-wide purchasing alliances responsible for individual patient care.

A new system must also reduce administrative costs. In the 1990s, fifteen hundred insurance companies competed for our health care dollars, producing huge redundancies and complexities in administrative and advertising costs. Moreover, these companies largely competed, not in matters of price and quality, but in the arts of "cherry-picking" customers who are less likely to fall sick or of designing benefits packages that limit the claims of those who do fall sick.

Efficiency must be defined with a wise heart, not just a calculator. Medical "cookbooks" should not limit providers; society should encourage them to adopt wise treatment guidelines. Inevitably, controlling costs requires respecting distinctions between needs and wants, effectiveness and futility, and setting priorities among health care needs. Efficiency in the service of universal access is a virtue, not a liability. It can offer choices and opportunities for health care for all people, instead of denying choice to millions. We must allocate our resources wisely so that we can achieve the goals of our health care system and address our other national needs.

3. *Health care is a public good.* Thus a good system must help increase our sense of responsibility, both as providers and as consumers. A huge social investment has helped to educate health care professionals and sustain the good they offer. Federal outlays for research and medical education, patients who offer their bodies to let young residents practice on them as they learn their art, community chest drives, foundation gifts, corporate grants, municipal taxes, bonds

floated to build hospitals—all these social supports confound the notion that health care is exclusively a private skill or a commodity up for grabs by the highest bidder. A society that recognizes and honors the social derivation of health care cannot plausibly reduce the distressed patient to a mere profit opportunity or to an object of hit or miss charity.

The indebtedness of professionals vastly exceeds the loans or fellowships they have received. Recognizing that they are not self-made, thousands of young professionals want to give back, even as they have received. The health care system must foster ways in which practitioners can make good on their profession as a calling, not just a job. The system must protect the integrity of professional judgment, weed out the incompetent or unethical practitioner, and encourage excellence.

The success of a health care system also depends on an increased sense of responsibility on the part of patients. We cannot solve our problems through a social mechanism alone. The success or failure of a system depends on the "habits of the heart" of a citizenry. Patients must be active partners in their health care. Preventing a heart attack, rehabilitating a spinal injury, coping with a stroke—these often require changes in the patients' habits. The system cannot gratify all wants, tamp down all worries, or remove the mark of mortality from our frame. We need some self-control over our wants, some composure in the midst of illness, and some courage in the face of dying. No system of itself can bring these virtues to us. We need to bring them to the system so that its benefits may sustain us more fully.

The ancient Romans tended to emphasize the benefits of citizenship; the Athenians emphasized its responsibilities. For its moral and economic success, the reform of our system of health care requires both.

These three foundational judgments about the good of health care and their derivative moral principles do not lie together in easy tranquillity. Tensions will inevitably arise between paying for the fundamental good of health care and providing for other basic goods (and relatively trivial commodities). The goals of universal and comprehensive coverage will also confront the hurdle of those start-up costs that major changes in either government or business inevitably entail, whatever the eventual economies achieved by reform. Differences will surely develop over priorities in goals, if not over the goals themselves, and over the best mechanisms and institutions by which to reach even agreed-on goals.

But critics can exaggerate the conflicts between principles and exploit this exaggeration to discredit truly comprehensive reform in favor of very restricted, incremental reform. For example, some members of Congress, fearing that universal coverage costs too much, have proposed only a few limited steps to increase access to care, such as requiring insurance companies to accept patients with pre-existing conditions. This specific reform, they believe, would help us along the way to universal coverage without the burden of mandated premiums, large tax subsidies, and governmental takeover and bureaucratization of health care.

Such partial reforms, however, can be counterproductive and eventually more costly. If, for example, one forces insurance companies to accept patients with pre-existing conditions ($100,000 cases are not unusual) without other coordinated measures, insurance companies will promptly raise the rates they charge the insured. In effect, costs will rise and shift from applicants with pre-existing conditions to the already insured. Almost as promptly, employers who have previously covered their employees will find reasons to drop this more expensive fringe benefit, and young and healthy employees will not pick up coverage on their own. The net result? In the absence of other coordinated measures, this otherwise very good reform will likely move the country farther from universal coverage through a scheme advertised to bring us closer to it. We will also exacerbate the current frenzy of cost shifting, which unfairly distributes the burdens of paying for health care and leads to increased costs, as the uninsured often delay going to a doctor or a hospital until they require expensive services. It is not self-evident that partial reforms best serve the total ecology of a health care system.

What about the political chances of passing major new health care legislation in this millennium? Will we be willing to make significant changes in the foreseeable future? My tragic law of politics goes as follows: The perception of a problem and the readiness to do something about it rarely surfaces before the solution is beyond reach. We could have reformed the health care system much more easily when Harry Truman said we needed to do it in 1948 and when health care costs were 4½ percent of the GNP. The amount was large, but relatively marginal to our total GNP. However, today health care costs have risen past 14 percent of the GNP; and 11 million people have jobs in the industry, some of them ready to attack changes that might affect their interests. Gridlocks in government usually reflect gridlocks of various kinds of interest groups in the society at large. Undoubtedly, public backing for major health care reform also depends in part on the state of the economy. The economy must not be so bad that the country feels it cannot afford the start-up costs of reform, but not so good that currently insured workers in their euphoria no longer worry about the loss of their jobs and with it their (admittedly diminishing) health care coverage.

However, I am not unrelievedly pessimistic. Sixty percent of U.S. voters have at one time or another said they would consider some rise in taxes in order to provide universal coverage. Politics, as Max Weber once put it, is, at best, slow boring through hard wood. Political solutions are *possible* but *difficult*—a good deal more difficult than my fellow Texan, Ross—just-lift-up-the-hood-and-fix-it—Perot is willing to admit.

To achieve major reform, we cannot treat health care simply as a partisan or an interest-group issue. We need to return to our foundations as a people. Our founders assumed that if a nation could create a common good it should make that good common. We can now deliver health care to all our people, and this good will help secure and enhance the life, liberty, and welfare that is our nation's promise to its citizens. It is time to reconfirm that promise to one another. Such a renewal of a covenant seems difficult, coming, as it does, so late in the day and with well-established interests already in the field. It will surely require a broad appeal to self-interest. But it will also need to appeal to what Lincoln called "the better angels of our nature," those angels that De Tocqueville must have discerned when he wrote that a "covenant exists . . . between all the citizens of a democracy when they all feel themselves subject to the same weakness and the same dangers; their interests as well as their compassion makes it a rule with them to lend one another assistance when required."

## A Theological Postscript

This chapter did not begin with a Christian justification for health care reform on the grounds that this placement might mislead. It might link too deductively Christian theological affirmations with the three "foundations" for a health care system, a link that might lead to several errors. It might leave too little room for good faith differences between Christians, if not on foundations and derivative principles, certainly on their relative weight. This loss of reflective space might, in turn, leave too little room for subsequent theological criticism of a particular design and its institutional realization. It might also imply that only Christians could arrive at these foundations, a restriction difficult to justify. One need not hold to the Christian faith to affirm health care as a fundamental and public good among other such goods.

At the same time, this chapter required at some point reflection on the theological tradition as it bears on the question of health care reform. Otherwise, I would, by implication, yield to those secularists and religionists who would distance religion from politics to the enfeeblement of the first and the impoverishment of both.

The secular objections to religious involvement in health care reform are familiar enough. Some secular participants in the debate over health care reform would like to keep religious language out of the discussion altogether. They appeal to the principle of the separation of church and state or fear the divisiveness of religious language in the political arena.

Both secular reasons for removing religious language from the public arena are too indiscriminate. Undoubtedly, the First Amendment prohibits the enactment of laws for purely religious *purposes*, such as the establishment or advancement of a particular religious tradition, but the First Amendment hardly intends to deny to citizens religious *motives* and *reasons* for believing and acting and voting as they do on matters of public purpose and the common good. Nor does it deny them the right to explain these motives and reasons to others. The amendment does not confine religious liberty purely to the private sphere. This restriction would flagrantly overlook the careful location of religious liberty in the First Amendment, among the freedoms of speech, assembly, and the press. These four liberties belong together in that they are not purely private liberties. Each supplies the means by which people assemble together through the spoken and written word to deliberate and reach their judgments on matters of great moment. As William Lee Miller has observed in *The First Liberty*, the founders clustered the four liberties in the First Amendment in order to undergird the deliberative process in a republic.[1] They wanted to insure the health and vigor of public discussion and debate about questions of the common good. To protect the deliberative process, the amendment forbids any legislative, executive, or judicial action that would establish a particular religious tradition over others or over those citizens who reject religious belief. But the amendment does not single out and deny to religious communities the right to participate in deliberations about the common good, which the other liberties, therein sited, so obviously also enable.

Others fear that religious language is inherently divisive and therefore unsuitable for discourse about common political purposes. It too quickly excludes those who are not in the know. This fear, however, flies in the face of Lincoln's appeal to religious language in helping the nation recover its badly shattered unity toward the end of the Civil War. In Lincoln's time and in our own, we misread the politics of the nation if we assume that we are indeterminately a public, religious or secular. Rather, the health of the nation depends on recognizing that, in forging national policies, we must appeal to publics within a public, among them religious publics, with their own particular memories, beliefs, and motives for action, which bear on questions of public purpose.

Two forms of the Christian tradition itself generate a still further reluctance to enter into debate on such public issues as health care reform. Sectarians tend to despair of the general social and political order altogether and would restrict the moral mandates of the faith to the formation of a distinctive Christian culture cut off from its surroundings. They would renounce the effort to engage the society at large in the question of bettering its institutional forms, and they despair of coalitions between religious communities and other publics. Their dismissal reminds me of the comment of the nineteenth-century Bishop of Chichester whose amiable stroll down the street with a friend was interrupted by two men, arguing with each other from open windows on opposite sides of the road. Those men will never agree, the Bishop said, they are arguing from opposite premises.

Sectarians believe that the church and other communities in the society at large cannot work for common ends without compromising the purity of the church's life and message. In effect, they can imagine only two ways in which the church might relate to the social and political order: either by a Constantinian domination of the world, with all the attendant dangers of corrupting the church's substance, or by a strict separation from the world for the sake of the Church's pure witness to a kingdom not of this earth. The sectarian worries that the loaf of bread compromises the yeast; the yeast does not leaven the loaf.

The second Christian reluctance springs not from sectarian denial of the world, but from a Lutheran modesty about the church's role in the political order. Gilbert Meilaender in *Faith and Faithfulness* offers an apt contemporary statement of this position. He limits the church's social and political action to interventions of two sorts: first, only occasional, negative, prophetic judgments against the political order for egregious wrongs (such as Nazi genocide policies) and, second, small-scale corporal works of mercy that the church directly undertakes (such as those enunciated in Isa. 61:1–2 and 58:6, which Jesus cites at the beginning of his ministry, or those tests of righteousness, which he sets forth in his parable on the Last Judgment, Matthew 25). Beyond that, the church keeps its voice out of politics. This Lutheran approach, while respecting the church's distinctive role, insufficiently honors, in my judgment, the degree to which the Gospel itself, although not supplying us with the templates for political institutions, does furnish us narratively with the basis for standards by which our imperfect work in the arena of politics may be measured.

## Access to the Healing Pool

Scripture does not use the language of modern debate. The narratives of the New Testament in koine Greek are mercifully free of Latinate tags—universal, comprehensive, and the like. But neither do such words force the narratives.

A story in the Gospel of John provides a parable for a health care system that gives access to all. John reports that an ill man had sought healing at the waters of Bethesda. But he finds the pool crowded on all sides, his access to the waters blocked. Jesus singles out this man, long excluded from the pool, and tells him, "Stand up, take your mat and walk."

> Now in Jerusalem by the Sheep Gate there is a pool, called in Hebrew Beth-zatha, which has five porticos. In these lay many invalids—blind, lame, and paralyzed. One man was there who had been ill for thirty-eight years. When Jesus saw him lying and knew that he had been there a long time, he said to him, "Do you want to be made well?" The sick man answered him, "Sir, I have no one to put me into the pool when the water is stirred up; and while I am making my way, someone else steps ahead of me. Jesus said to him, "Stand up, take your mat and walk." At once the man was made well and he took up his mat and began to walk. (John 5: 2–9).

Through many such stories, the Gospels emphasize the outreach and the scope of Jesus' ministry as a healer. He heals the outsiders, those who do not have access to the good of healing; and his healing takes diverse forms depending on need. He cleanses lepers; he breaks the hold of demonic and destructive powers that assault the afflicted; and he restores still others to bodily integrity as he empowers them to see, hear, and walk.

These stories both feature the savior as the healer of illness and also serve as signs of the larger work of redemption accomplished through his coming and the inauguration of God's reign. Jesus' healing miracles are not haphazard. They fall into three types: miracles that cleanse, that liberate from demonic and destructive power, and that restore the sufferer to bodily integrity and health. Together, these several types of healing serve as signs of the cleansing, liberating, and restorative work that God accomplishes through Jesus' ministry, death, and resurrection.[2]

Still, although the miracles point beyond the healing episodes to the larger saving work of God, they also say something directly and immediately about the human good of health and the work of healing. Health is a fundamental, not a trivial, good. Men and women instinctively, urgently, and passionately seek it out. They thirst for healing as for water. Thus the place of healing, like water in the desert, quickly becomes a public place. Healing is a public good, and only too quickly a scarce public good. But the savior-healer swiftly reaches out to those who have no access to the good and extends it to them, the resourceless, the needy, those with no money to put into the stile, no insurance card to flash their way into the hospital, no motorized wheelchair to bring them up to the edge of the healing waters. Were health and healing trivial goods, exclusion would not matter. But healing is a fundamental good, and therefore it should reach everybody: All should have access to the healing pool. Health care coverage should be universal.

The diversity of Jesus' miracles also recognizes that healing itself is diverse. The needs of the sick vary, and therefore health care itself must be diverse, that is, comprehensive. Jesus does not heal the lame, at the expense of the halt and the blind, or the deaf, at the expense of the scurveyed and the tormented. Indeed, to be universal, health care must also be comprehensive.

To reach all those in need, it must address the full range of needs.

The importance of the notion of universality and the intimate connection between universality and comprehensiveness show up in the later doctrine of the "catholicity" of the church. The ancient creedal affirmation of the church as catholic traces back to scripture. The New Testament takes care to treat Jesus' works of healing as signs. They do not simply serve as a basket of goods that temporarily meet needs; they point beyond themselves to a supreme good, which Jesus himself inaugurates and incarnates. More-over, the church believed that this supreme good, the self-expending love of God, must reach everybody. This belief informed that strangely urgent missionary impulse that has characterized Christianity from the beginning. "Go into all the nations and baptize them. . . ." Later in history, this missionary impulse to spread, rather than to hoard, the supreme good strayed from the exuberant love that originally propelled it. The missionary impulse distorted into the urge to conquer, to rule, to coerce, and to exploit. But the original impulse arose from a sense that the supreme good, the ultimate good, belongs to no one; it should divide no one from others; it should not divide humankind into the haves and the have nots. Indeed, a reluctance to share this supreme good would surely betray a want of love.

Thus the early church used the word "catholicity" to describe one of its primary marks apart from which the church defected from its mission. "Catholicity" referred to the church's "universality." The church seized on the image of the ark to describe its universal mission. It is an "ark of salvation" open to all creatures, familiar and strange, beautiful and grotesque, irrespective of shape, color, size, gender, wealth, and age. Societies may organize themselves into the rich and poor, the haves and have nots, but the church, as bearer of the supreme good, must, at least in principle, make the Word and sacraments available to all who confess their need.

Derivatively and analogously, fundamental goods such as health care—goods less than supreme, but still fundamental to human life and flourishing—should reach all in need. The services of physicians and others in the helping professions should extend beyond the parochial, restricting, and excluding boundaries that ordinary life establishes. These life- and health-serving goods should extend to the stranger and the needy. A profession corrupts if it becomes captive to the interests of a particular class. Physicians and nurses, and the society that arranges for their services, lose much that belongs to their moral substance if they merely hire out in contracts to serve a single class, if they lose the mark, as it were, of "catholicity."

Furthermore, theologians eventually distinguished between two dimensions of the church's catholicity: external and internal. Its external catholicity refers to the church's mission to reach the whole of humankind, to what we have already identified as the church's universality. Its internal catholicity refers to the church's obligation to meet the needs of the whole person, body and soul. (The Catholic theologian Karl Adam, for example, argued that an overly intellectual Protestantism emphasized the preaching of the Word at the expense of other ingredients in worship that address the senses of sight, sound, and smell.)[3]

Correspondingly, in distributing the fundamental good of health care, we must not only meet the needs of the whole public (the standard of universality) but also address the whole needs of the public (the standard of comprehensiveness). If the first obligation requires that the health care system reaches everybody, the second requires the development of the full manifold of services needed; that is, preventive, rehabilitative, long-term, and terminal care, as well as acute care; treatment for mental, as well as physical, illness. These standards are distinct, but related. When a profession or a system fails to develop a full range of services, it also fails to reach the entire population in need.

The scriptural narratives make a second point about healing with implications for a health care system. Although healing is a fundamental good, it is not the only fundamental good, nor does it rank with the supreme good to which the acts of healing point. At the beginning of his ministry, Jesus reads the passage from Isaiah,

> The Spirit of the Lord is upon me,
> Because he has anointed me to bring
>     good news to the poor.
> He has sent me to proclaim release to the captives
> And recovery of sight to the blind,
> To let the oppressed go free,
> To Proclaim the year of the Lord's favor.
> —Isaiah 61:1–2

This passage points to a series of other fundamental goods on which the full flourishing of a community and its members depends: healing, but also food, clothing, and shelter for the poor, and justice for captives and the oppressed.

Furthermore, these several goods are but the signs of a supreme good at hand. Health and healing are goods that derive from God; they signify the imminent work of God; but they themselves are not God. Their

status has implications for piety and policy. The goodness of healing authorizes us to pray for it and commit
resources to it. But healing is not the sole good or the
chief good, and therefore we cannot pray for it—or
fund it—as though health and health care alone matter. We are authorized to pray for life and healing, but
not too desperately. Jesus prayed, "Father, let this cup
pass from me, nevertheless, not my will but thine be
done."

This scriptural placement of healing in the setting
of other goods suggests that health care ought not
crowd out budgetary support for other fundamental
goods in the total economy of a society. The rapidly
increasing cost of health care since World War II in
the United States makes it clear that the economic
question of cost effectiveness is a moral question of
properly honoring and balancing priorities; and, in
the background of the economic and moral questions,
lies the religious question of stewardship. How do we
distribute the fundamental good of health care uni-
versally and comprehensively, and yet prudently and
efficiently enough so as to honor our responsibilities
to other goods? Religiously considered, policy mak-
ers, providers, and recipients of health care, in differing ways, are stewards of goods received, not wholly
their own.

Scripture does not provide us with a scheme or
design for producing, balancing, and distributing basic
goods, but it strikes the great themes we need to work
through in our common life together. In my judgment,
we wrongly diminish the scope of these scriptural
themes if we restrict the church's role and voice to
delivering corporal works of mercy and withdraw altogether from the arena of politics, as though God's
grace penetrates the sphere of the personal and the

intimate alone. The logic of God's corporal works of mercy requires efforts at institutional reform. Nurturing institutions—even of the tax-supported variety—may sometimes intimate and foreshadow the kingdom of God. By the same token, we would also restrict the role and scope of medical ethics if we reflected at length and painstakingly on the subject of the covenanted physician but neglected the larger structural issues of health care reform.

# Notes

## Introduction

1. George Lakoff and Mark Johnson, *Metaphor We Live By* (University of Chicago Press, 1980), p. 5. "The essence of metaphor is understanding and experiencing one thing through another."

2. For the quandary approach to ethics, see H. D. Aiken, "Levels of Moral Conduct," in H. D. Aiken (ed.), *Reason and Conduct: New Bearings in Moral Philosophy* (Greenwod Press, 1982). For its exemplary application to medical ethics, see Tom L. Beauchamp and James F. Childress, *Principles of Biomedical Ethics* (Oxford University Press, 1979). For its criticism, see Edmind Pincoffs, "Quandary Ethics," *Mind* 80 (1971): pp. 552–571; Stanley Hauerwas, *Vision and Virtue* (Fides Publishers, 1974); Stanley Hauerwas et al., *Truthfulness and Tragedy* (University of Notre Dame Press, 1977); and Alasdair MacIntyre, *After Virtue* (University of Notre Dame Press, 1981).

3. Lakoff and Johnson, *Metaphors We Live By*, Ch. 3, pp. 10–13. Professor James Childress of the University of Virginia first drew my attention to this helpful book.

4. Ibid.

5. Paul Ricoeur, *The Symbolism of Evil*, tr. by Emerson Buchan (Beacon Press, 1969).

6. Lakoff and Johnson, "Metaphorical Systematicity: Highlighting and Hiding," *Metaphors We Live By*, pp. 10–13.

7. Gerardus van der Leeuw, *Religion in Essence and Manifestation*, tr. By J. E. Turner (George Allen & Unwin, 1938), p. 219.

8. Mircea Eliade, *From Medicine Men to Muhammad* (Harper & Row, 1974), pp. 3–4. (Part 4 of his *From Primitives to Zen*; Harper & Row, 1967.) See also Mircea Eliade, *Shamanism:*

*Archaic Techniques of Ecstasy*, tr. by Willard Trask (Princeton University Press, 1964).

9. Leon R. Kass, "Regarding the End of Medicine and the Pursuit of Health," *The Public Interest* 40 (National Affairs, Inc., 1975).

10. Herbert Benson, M.D., *The Relaxation Response* (Avon Books, 2000).

11. Most of these phrases appear in Herbert Benson, M.D., *Timeless Healing: The Power and Biology of Belief* (Simon & Schuster, 1996).

12. Herbert Benson, *Timeless Healing*, suggests that the medicine of the future will resemble a three-legged stool (self-care, meditations, and procedures); spiritual techniques largely serve the task of self-care.

13. Data reported by D. A. Matthews, D. B. Larson, and C. P. Barry in *The Faith Factor: An Annotated Bibliography of Clinical Research on Spiritual Subjects*, vol. 1 (John Templeton Foundation, 1994) and summarized in Herbert Benson, *Timeless Healing*, pp. 173–75.

14. Charles Marwick reported this recommendation as issuing from the first conference on spiritual dimensions in clinical research: "Should Physicians Prescribe Prayer for Health? Spiritual Aspects of Well-being Considered," *JAMA* 273 (1995): 1561–62.

15. R. P. Sloan et al., "Religion, Spirituality, and Medicine," *Lancet* 353 (1999): 664–67.

16. E. Brooks Holifield, *Health and Medicine in the Methodist Tradition: Journey toward Wholeness* (Crossroad, 1986).

17. Joseph C. Rheingold, *The Mother, Anxiety, and Death: The Catastrophic Death Complex* (Little, Brown & Co., 1967), p. 228.

## 1. Parent

1. Willa Cather, *Five Stories* (Vintage Books, 1956), p. 104.

2. *Works of Martin Luther*, Philadelphia Edition, ed. by Henry E. Jacobs, Vol. 2 (Muhlenburg Press, 1915), pp. 356, 360, 361.

3. Alexander Solzhenitsyn, *Cancer Ward* (Bantam Books, 1969), Chs. 5 and 7, especially p. 54.

4. For an extensive description of this looping behavior in total institutions, see Erving Goffman, "On the Characteristics of Total Institutions, " in his *Asylums: Essays on the Social Situation of Mental and Other Inmates* (Doubleday & Co., Anchor Books, 1961), pp. 1–123; and David Rothman, *The Discovery of the Asylum: Social Order and Disorder in the New Republic* (Little, Brown

& Co., 1971), or, better yet, Nurse Ratchet in the movie version of Ken Kesey's *One Flew over the Cuckoo's Nest*.

5. John Stuart Mill, *On Liberty* (Appleton-Century-Crofts, 1947), p. 76.

6. Brian Clark, *Whose Life Is It Anyway?* (Avon Books, 1978), p. 28.

7. Ibid., p. 98.

8. Ibid., p. 99.

9. Arthur Caplan and Daniel Callahan (eds.), *Ethics in Hard Times* (Plenum, 1981), pp. 261–81.

10. Joel Feinberg draws the distinction between "weak" and "strong" paternalism—the first referring to the restriction of nonvoluntary choices; the second to the restriction of voluntary choices; see "Legal Paternalism," *Canadian Journal of Philosophy* 1 (Dec. 1971): 105–24.

11. Fyodor Dostoevsky, *The Brothers Karamazov* (Random House, Modern Library, 1952), p. 269.

12. Ibid., p. 271.

13. Dan W. Brock of Brown University, in a paper presented at the Kennedy Institute of Ethics, Georgetown University, Oct. 27, 1981, on "Paternalism and Promoting the Good," published in *Paternalism*, Rolf Sartorius (ed.), (University of Minnesota Press, 1983).

## 2. Fighter

1. Albert Camus, *The Plague*, tr. by Stuart Gilbert (Hamish Hamilton, 1948), p. 123. See also Albert Camus, *The Myth of Sisyphus and Other Essays*, tr. by Justin O'Brien (Alfred A. Knopf, 1955), and *The Rebel*, tr. by Anthony Bower (Vintage Books, 1956), his novel *The Stranger*, tr. by Stuart Gilbert (Vintage Books, 1946), and his play *The Just Assassins, in Caligula and Three Other Plays*, tr. by Stuart Gilbert (Alfred A. Knopf, 1958).

2. Diana Crane, *The Sanctity of Social Life: Physicians' Treatment of Critically Ill Patients* (Russell Sage Foundation, 1979).

3. *Historical Statistics of the U.S., Part I* (U.S. Bureau of the Census, 1975), p. 319; and Daniel R. Waldo (ed.), *Health Care Financing Trends* 3, no. 1 (June 1982): 2.

4. Gerardus van der Leeuw, *Religion in Essence and Manifestation*, tr. by J. E. Turner (George Allen & Unwin, 1938), pp. 468–69.

5. Arthur C. McGill, the author of *Suffering: A Test of Theological Method* (The Westminster Press, 1982), offered these

comments about death and suffering in a plenary address before
the American Academy of Religion, 1974.

6. It is doubtful whether the perception of either death or suffering as absolute evil controls decisions consistently and deductively in all areas. It would be surprising, for example, if
pro-lifers were invariably opponents of the Vietnam War. In
the 1980s, however, some Catholic bishops have argued that a
pro-life position on abortion has its policy implications for the
church's position on nuclear war.

7. Eric Cassell, *The Healer's Art* (Penguin Books, 1979), Ch. 7.

8. Recall, for instance, Chevy Chase's news bulletins on the struggle to keep Generalissimo Franco alive: The effort to prolong
life extended beyond the humiliating to the ridiculous.

9. "Optimum Care for Hopelessly Ill Patients: A Report of the
Clinical Care Committee of the Massachusetts General Hospital," *New England Journal of Medicine* 295 (Aug. 12, 1976):
362–64.

10. Paul Ramsey, *The Patient as Person* (Yale University Press,
1970), p. 133.

11. Ibid., p. 133. Professor Ramsey exercises care to show how some
Roman Catholic moralists (e.g., Gerald Kelly, S. J.) have taken
steps, albeit cautious, in the direction of his views. Physicians
tend to distinguish between ordinary and heroic measures, on
the basis of status of the means used. Recent interpreters of the
Roman Catholic distinction between ordinary and extraordinary means are more inclined to include the condition of the
patient and not just the status of the means as factors in decision
making. Although Fr. Kelly carefully hedges his remarks, he recognizes circumstances under which a means as ordinary as water
may be inappropriate. For this reason, my criticisms in this section have been chiefly directed against the distinction as the
medical community rather than contemporary Christian moralists usually formulate it.

12. As written, the document requires that the physician consult
with and secure the concurrence of the family only in the decision to perform certain acts of commission (such as turning off
a patient's mechanical ventilator) that will lead to death. It is my
understanding, however, that in actual practice the MGH staff
regularly consults with the patient and/or family.

13. Mitchell T. Rabkin, M.D.et al., "Orders Not to Resuscitate,"
*New England Journal of Medicine* 295 (Aug. 12, 1976): 364–66.

14. Joseph Fletcher, *Morals and Medicine* (1954; Princeton University Press, 1979), Ch. 6.

15. Joanne Lynn, M.D., "Supportive Care for Dying Patients," Appendix B in *Deciding to Forego Life-Sustaining Treatment*, a volume prepared by the President's Commission for the study of Ethical Problems in Medicine and Biomedical and Behavioral Research (U.S. Government Printing Office, 1983), pp. 275–97.

16. Quoted by Peter Steinfels in *The New York Times*, February 14, 1993, Section 4, pp. 1, 6.

17. *The New York Times*, January 25, 1993.

18. Cited by Richard A. McCormick, S.J., "Physician Assisted Suicide: Flight from Compassion," *Christian Century*, December 4, 1991, p. 1133.

19. See Søren Kierkegaard, *Thoughts on Crucial Situations in Human Life*, tr. by David F. Swenson (Augsburg Publishing House, 1941).

20. For what follows, see Philippe Aries, *Western Attitudes toward Death* (John Hopkins University Press, 1974).

21. Geoffrey Gorer, *Death, Grief, and Mourning* (1965; Arno Press, 1977).

## 3. Technician

1. John Stuart Mill, *Utilitarianism* (Bobbs-Merrill Co., 1957), p. 22.

2. Immanuel Kant, *Groundwork of the Metaphysics of Morals*, tr. by H. J. Paton (Harper & Row, Harper Torchbooks, 1964), p. 82.

3. Ibid.

4. Rudyard Kipling, *Rudyard Kipling's Verse: Definitive Edition* (Doubleday & Co., 1940), p. 123.

5. Ibid.

6. Ibid., p. 125. The same orchestral image dominates Kipling's short story "The Ship That Found Herself" (1895), in which the captain of a steamship explains to the owner's daughter that the ship she has just christened will not be a real ship until tested in storm at sea—when all the parts have a chance to work together—"sweetenin' her, we call it technically."

7. Pedro Lain Entralgo, *Doctor and Patient*, tr. by Frances Partridge (McGraw-Hill Book Co., 1969), pp. 21–23.

8. "Obligations of Patients to Their Physicians," *Code of Medical Ethics*, Ch. 1, Art. 11, American Medical Association, May 1847 (American Medical Association Press, 1897).

9. Ernest Hemingway, "In Our Time," in *Hemingway* (Viking Press, Viking Portable Library, 1949), p. 442.

10. Ernest Hemingway, "Bull Fighting a Tragedy," *The Toronto Star Weekly*, Oct. 20, 1923, in William White (ed.), *By-Line: Ernest Hemingway* (Charles Scribner's Sons, 1967), pp. 90–108.

11. Ibid.

12. Eric Cassell, *The Healer's Art* (Penguin Books, 1979).

13. For the most sustained development of the distinction between the two ways of looking at the work of art, see Meyer H. Abrams, *The Mirror and the Lamp* (Oxford University Press, 1953).

14. See Andre Malraux, *The Voices of Silence*, tr. by Stuart Gilbert (Doubleday & Co., 1953), for a romantic, almost Nietzschean celebration of the artist's godlike creativity.

15. Cassell, *The Healer's Art*, p. 48.

## 4. The Physician's Covenant

1. William Faulkner, "Delta Autumn," in *Go Down Moses* (Vintage Books, 1973), p. 351.

2. Ibid., pp. 350–51.

3. Ibid., p. 354.

4. Ludwig Edelstein, *Ancient Medicine*, ed. by Owsei Temkin and C. Lilian Temkin (Johns Hopkins Press, 1967), pp. 40–48.

5. Ibid., p. 6.

6. Ibid.

7. "American Medical Association—First Code of Medical Ethics" (1847), in Stanley J. Reiser et al. (eds.), *Ethics in Medicine: Historical Perspectives and Contemporary Concerns* (MIT Press, 1977), p. 30, Sect. 2, Art. 11.

8. Ibid., p. 34, Sect. 3, Art. 11.

9. Ibid., p. 29, Sect. 1, Art. 1.

10. Published in *The New York Times*, June 6, 1975, Op-Ed page.

11. See, for example, Henry Sumner Maine, *Ancient Law*, rev. ed. (Oxford University Press, 1931).

12. Richard M. Titmuss, *The Gift Relationship: From Human Blood to Social Policy* (Pantheon Books, 1971).

13. Robert M. Veatch, *A Theory of Medical Ethics* (Basic Books, 1981).

14 William F. May, "Code, Covenant, Contract or Philanthropy," *Hastings Center Report* 5 (Dec. 1975): 29–38.

15. John Rawls, *A Theory of Justice* (Harvard University Press, 1971).

16. Roderick Firth, "Ethical Absolutism and the Ideal Observer Theory," *Philosophy and Phenomenological Research* 12 (1952): 317–45.

17. Veatch is willing to use the words "contract" and "covenant" interchangeably, but he ignores the differences that a religious setting makes. His theory tilts in the direction of the view of contract generally available through John Rawls.

18. The earlier contractarians, Hobbes and Locke, differ from the Rawls/Veatch version of contractarian thought. They never asked us to engage in a thought project that prescinds from the fact of evil. In fact, they see the state as arising purely as a defensive reaction to the fact of evil, the threat of theft, murder, and violent battle. Criticism of this line of contractarian thought takes a different tack, which I tried to explore in an essay, "Adversarialism in America and the Professions," *Center Magazine* 14, no. 1 (Jan.-Feb. 1981): 47–58.

19. Paul Ramsey of Princeton University, following the theologian Karl Barth, first applied the term "covenant fidelity" to the problems of medical ethics in this country in his impressive and influential *The Patient as Person* (Yale University Press, 1970). As brilliantly, however, as Ramsey marks out the ramifications of the moral ideal for decision making, he spends only two pages in the preface (pp. xii and xiii) acknowledging the theological origins of the notion. Without a firm sense of the religious setting for covenant (that reckons with suffering and death in the context of the divine fidelity), the moral ideal of fidelity fades before the exigencies of the real world or threatens merely to torture the unduly conscientious.

20. Leon R. Kass, "Regarding the End of Medicine and the Pursuit of Health," *Public Interest* 40 (Summer 1975): 27–29.

21. Eliot Freidson, *Professional Dominance: The Social Structure of Medical Care* (Atherton Press, 1970), p. 94.

## 5. Teacher

1. Carter L. Marshall, "Prevention and Health Education," in *Maxcy-Rosenau Public Health and Preventive Medicine*, 11th ed., ed. by John M. Last et al. (Appleton-Century-Crofts, 1980), pp. 1114–15.

2. Duncan Neuhauser, "Don't Teach Preventive Medicine: A Contrary View," *Public Health Reports* 97 (May–June 1982): 222.

3. Ibid., p. 221.

4. Ibid.
5. Horacio Fabrega, "Concepts of Disease: Logical Features and Social Implications," *Perspectives in Biology and Medicine* 15 (Summer 1972): 605–15.
6. Marshall Becker and Louis Maiman, "Strategies for Enhancing Patient Compliance," *Journal for Community Health* 6 (Winter 1980): 113.
7. Ibid., p. 114.
8. Søren Kierkegaard, *The Concept of Dread*, tr. by Walter Lowrie (Princeton University Press, 1944), pp. 110–15.
9. Becker and Maiman, "Strategies for Enhancing Patient Compliance," p. 119.
10. Ibid., pp. 127–29.
11. Marshall, "Prevention and Health Education," p. 1114.
12. Daniel R. Waldo (ed.), *Health Care Financing Trends* 3, no. 1 (June 1982): 2.
13. Marshall, "Prevention and Health Education," p. 1114.
14. W. Hutchinson, "Health Insurance: On Our Financial Relation to the Public," *Journal of the American Medical Association* 7 (Oct. 30, 1886): 477–81. Quoted by Duncan Neuhauser, "Don't Teach Preventive Medicine," p. 222.
15. Samuel L. Feder, "Attitudes of Patients with Advanced Malignancy," in *Death and Dying: Attitudes of Patient and Doctor*, Symposium no. 11, Group for the Advancement of Psychiatry (Mental Health Materials Center, 1965), p. 619.
16. Abraham Flexner, *Medical Education in the United States and Canada* (1910; repr. Arno Press, 1972).

## 6. Covenanted Institutions

1. John Cheever, *Oh What a Paradise It Seems* (Ballantine Books, 1982), p. 2.
2. Willard Gaylin and Daniel Callahan, "The Psychiatrist as Double Agent," *Hastings Center Report* 8 (April 1978): 1–23.
3. *The Model Code of Professional Responsibility* (American Bar Association, 1981), *Canon* 5 E C 23. The new model rules carry forward this prohibition implicitly rather than explicitly in Rule 5.3 C, *Model Rules of Professional Conduct* (American Bar Association, 1983).
4. Walter P. Metzger, "What Is a Profession?" *Seminar Reports*, Programs of General and Continuing Education in the Humanities 3, no. 1 (Columbia University, 1975).

5. Leo Tolstoy, *The Death of Ivan Ilych* (Signet Classics, 1960), p. 121.

6. Marna K. Carney, "Health Care for the Poor: Some Dilemmas," paper presented at the Kennedy Institute of Ethics, Georgetown University, Oct. 23, 1973 (unpublished), pp. 11–15.

## 7. A Covenanted Health Care System

1. William Lee Miller, *The First Liberty: Religion and the American Republic* (Alfred A. Knopf, 1986), "On the Underpinnings of Republicanism," pp. 343–53.

2. The healing miracles of cleansing serve as signs of God's forgiving love (justifying grace); the miracles of liberation and restoration point to God's empowering love (sanctifying grace). The tradition also recognized two aspects to sanctifying or empowering grace: the negative task of liberation from demonic power and the positive task of restoration to our full, intended powers. Together, these three aspects of grace reflect the saving work of Christ as summarized in the doctrine of the atonement: the forensic work of forgiveness, the military work of victory over destructive power, and the subjective work of restoration to our intended powers.

3. Karl Adam, *The Spirit of Catholicism* (Image Books, 1954), Ch. 9.

# Index

ence of the patient on the physician, 10–11; in ethics and Biblical setting, 28; family physician preserving the parental image, 29–58; fighter, physician in the face of disease and death, 27–28, and as healer, 4–6, 8; healer, 4–6, 8; medicine men and women, forerunners to the Images, 16, 19–22, 29–31; parental image, 25–26: role in corrective vision, 1–16; social meanings and understanding the healer's role, 4; sources of, 16–19, 23–25

Institutions, covenanted: 182–209; beyond the hospital, 202–205; bureaucracy in 184; clinics, 182, 204; ghetto hospital and home care, 189; health maintenance organizations, 202–5. *See also* Health Maintenance Organizations; Hospitals and clinics

Johnson, Mark and George Lakoff, 12–13

Kant, Immanuel, 14, 24; on ethic of duty, 89
Kass, Leon, 19, 140
Kierkegaard, Søren, 84, 163
Kipling, Rudyard, *McAndrew's Hymn*, 90–92
Kübler-Ross, Elisabeth, 16, 176: on healer as companion in death, 26–27; on quest for the human experience of dying, 66

Lakoff, George and Mark Johnson, 12–13
Larson, D. B., 21
Leeuw, Gerardus van der, 66
Luther, Martin, 35
Lynn, Joanne, on humane care, 82–83

McCaslin, Isaac, 112
MacGill, Arthur C., 67
Machiavelli, 15; on ethics as corrective vision, 3
Massachusetts General Hospital and Beth Israel Hospital, contrasting classification of critically ill patients, 73–88
Matthews, D. A., 21
Medical education, 182: schools to educate, hospitals to heal, 185–109, therapeutic impact of teaching, 7
Medical ethics: code of law for humankind, 97–98, 101–5; as corrective vision, 1, 3; creating image of shelter and rescue for the doctor, 15; philosophical ethics in fight against death, 10
Medicine men and women: contemporary religion and myth of restoration, 20–24; healing in the setting of a religious narrative, 16–18. *See also* Shamen and women
Meilaender, Gilbert, 227
Metzger, Walter P., 192–93
Miller, William Lee, 25

Niebuhr, Reinhold, *Moral Man and Immoral Society*, 196